THE LANDMARK **METHOD**
FOR
TEACHING WRITING

By Jean Gudaitis Tarricone, M.Ed.

Production of this publication was made possible
through funding from:

State Street Foundation
225 Franklin Street
Boston, Massachusetts

Landmark Foundation
P.O. Box 227
Prides Crossing, MA 01965
(978) 927-4440

(c) **2000** by Jean **Gudaitis Tarricone**, M.Ed. and
Landmark Foundation

Proceeds from the sale of this **publication** are
used to support Landmark Foundation
training programs.

Published by Landmark Foundation
P.O. Box 227
Prides Crossing, MA 0 1965

Library of Congress Cataloging
in **Publication** Data

Tarricone, Jean Gudaitis
The Landmark Method for Teaching Writing
LC 4704.85737   1995 37 **1.9'0446'23-dc20**

COPIES OF THIS PUBLICATION CAN BE
ORDERED BY **CONTACTING**:

Landmark Outreach Program
PO. Box 227, Prides Crossing, MA 01965
(978) 927-4440
ISBN O-9624 119-3-O

Printed in U.S.A. 10 9 8 7 6 5 4 3 2

Acknowledgements

The Landmark Outreach Program and I would like to thank the State Street Foundation/State Street Bank, 225 Franklin Street, Boston, Massachusetts for the generous grant they provided to fund the writing and publishing of this book. I would also like to extend my deepest appreciation to Mr. Nicholas Lopardo, current president of Landmark School's Board of Directors, for his invaluable assistance in this endeavor. His efforts will enable us to train more teachers than ever before in the area of writing. I would also like to thank Headmaster Robert Broudo for his consistent support of this and many other special projects at Landmark; his vision for the school is ever-expanding and for that I am grateful. Thanks also go to Joan Sedita and Anne Marie Carpenter, both of the Landmark Outreach Program, for their direction, research assistance, and general know-how during the production stages.

Special thanks must go to my colleagues within the academic program who not only gave me tremendous support during the writing of this book, but who have advised and encouraged me throughout my career. I would like to thank South Campus Director Christopher Murphy for his support and encouragement of this project and his unparalleled commitment to our school. His greatest talent is cultivating the talents of others; without his leadership, this book could not have been written. Also, I would like to thank Henry Willette, South Campus Academic Dean, for his support in giving me the extra time to work on this project. Special thanks must also be extended to Speech and Language Pathologists September Schofield and Linda Gross, who have taught me so much; I am lucky to have worked so closely with such knowledgeable and talented women. Special thanks go to Linda for proofreading drafts and offering valuable constructive criticism. I would also like to thank Diane Vener, Study Skills Department Head at South Campus, for always being there when I need her; her advice, suggestions, and offers of help are appreciated more than she knows. I would also like to thank various people involved in Landmark's Language Arts department over the years. All have taught and inspired me: Helen Bryant, Louise Ingalls, Carol Ann Dumond, Terry Jennings, and Suzanne Crossman. In particular, I would like to thank Suzanne for her compilation and development of Landmark's essay writing strategy; many students have benefitted from her work. Special thanks must also be extended to Landmark's Language Arts teachers, who have implemented many of these methods over the years; their feedback and refinement are what have made them so successful.

I also want to thank my wonderful husband, Louis, for his love and support throughout all my endeavors. I am constantly awed by how incredibly fortunate I am. Last, but certainly not least, I would like to thank my son, Nathan, who has added an indescribable dimension to my life. His birth coincided with the completion of this book, and I cannot think of a happier ending.

Jean Gudaitis Tarricone, M.Ed.
August 1995

CONTENTS

PREFACE

Landmark School, a program of the Landmark Foundation, is an internationally recognized private, not-for-profit, residential and day school serving children and adolescents, ages 7-21, with language-based learning disabilities/dyslexia. In addition to campuses in Massachusetts, on Boston's North Shore, the Foundation also directs Landmark West, a day school in Encino, California.

The curriculum of all Landmark programs emphasizes the development of skills in reading, spelling, composition, math and study skills. In addition, attention is given to subject-area classes such as social studies and science, in order to build both general knowledge and study skills. This methodology for teaching writing is based on Landmark School's extensive experience providing for and observing students in one-to-one tutorials and small classes.

In addition to remedial education, Landmark School is involved in teacher training, diagnosis, and research. The Landmark Outreach Program was founded in 1977 as the consulting branch of the Landmark Foundation. This program provides staff development and training, enabling classroom teachers outside of Landmark to respond more effectively to the needs of students experiencing a variety of learning problems. Over several years, Landmark Outreach has received numerous requests for information pertaining to Landmark methodologies. This book is, in large measure, a response to the need represented by those requests.

Additional Landmark publications include: *Landmark Study Skills Guide, Landmark Method for Teaching Mathematics*, and *Thematic Instruction: A Teacher's Primer for Developing Speaking and Writing Skills.*

INTRODUCTION

Landmark has been continuously refining its curriculum to find the best ways to teach students with language-based learning disabilities/dyslexia since the school's inception in 1970. Over the years, Landmark has made much progress in teaching literacy skills to students who have a history of failure in other academic settings. The writing curriculum that follows is one such example. It is the result of much work on the part of many professionals throughout the years. Some of the curriculum is based on the research and curriculum ideas of professionals outside the school. Many other parts have been largely adapted and even invented by Landmark teachers to suit their needs. This combination of research and direct application in the classroom has resulted in a highly effective writing curriculum for students who have not been able to write before.

This book is for teachers, parents, students, and learning disabled individuals. Since it is a curriculum guide with specific ideas and exercises for teaching writing, it is most applicable for a teacher in the classroom. It is also valuable for parents interested in basic techniques to help their child learn; parents can also share these ideas with their child's teacher. In addition, learning disabled individuals can gain a better understanding of their own learning style and the learning techniques that work best for them.

Most importantly, the techniques in this book can be adapted to meet specific needs. For example, teachers outside of Landmark School probably do not have small, homogeneously grouped classes (like at Landmark), or strict reinforcement of these writing skills across the curriculum. Teachers need to adapt this writing program to meet their needs and those of the students. They can take only specific pieces of it or glean Landmark's main ideas and redesign all specific exercises their own way. The main purpose of this book is to explain Landmark's methodologies and offer suggestions for teachers to improve their methodologies. Keeping this in mind will help teachers to use this book most effectively.

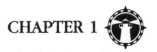

CHAPTER 1

Common Deficits
of the
Learning-Disabled Student

For students without language-based learning disabilities, a traditional school model, especially at the elementary grades, is not a particularly stressful experience. Children get to be with their friends each day, learn new information, conduct basic science experiments, learn how to spend money, and write and hear interesting stories. Most children easily handle these strongly language-mediated tasks within a regular curriculum; the speed and intensity with which the teacher introduces content and skills provide the correct challenge and motivational level.

For students with language deficits, these "simple," "fun" tasks can become major informational processing projects. Students may get lost in a sea of confusion, barely able to keep their heads above water. These seemingly easy tasks are actually laden with language demands that these children cannot handle without adequate structure and remediation. Some common deficits in children with language-based learning disabilities are described below.

Organizational Deficits

An organizational deficit is difficulty organizing information, both incoming and outgoing. Students may have difficulty processing both oral and written information and organizing time and materials. As a result, they cannot understand material presented or cannot effectively organize their thoughts to demonstrate true knowledge in oral and written situations.

Comprehension Deficits

Comprehension weaknesses are common among students with learning disabilities. They may occur in academic or social arenas. Students may have difficulty comprehending lectures, abstract concepts, or social situations that require them to perceive hidden motivations or implications. During the writing process, students may misperceive assignment instructions or be unable to provide the specificity and support necessary for a well-written piece.

General Processing Deficits

Many learning-disabled students have difficulty processing auditory and visual information. These deficits can contribute to the organizational and comprehension deficits. Children's inability to decipher, store, and retrieve information properly can impede the writing process. Since these children have difficulty deciphering presented material, they cannot decide what or how to write.

Language Deficits

Students who have difficulty processing language have trouble in many or all of the areas mentioned above. In the written realm, language deficits can lead to problems with word retrieval and semantic and syntactical awareness. Children who have difficulty accessing vocabulary and constructing basic sentence types have difficulty with any writing assignment.

Memory Deficits

Since learning-disabled students have trouble processing, storing, and retrieving information, both long- and short-term memory may be affected. Shortly after learning something, children may behave as if they never heard the information before; or, they may be unable to apply the information to a new situation. Therefore, they may not be able to complete homework or other tasks because they forget how after only a few hours.

Motor Deficits

Problems with fine or gross motor skills are common in learning-disabled children. Fine motor problems may be manifested in poor handwriting, an inability to copy detailed visual materials, or difficulty manipulating hands-on materials. Gross motor problems may produce general "clumsiness" or difficulty with athletic activities.

Higher-Order Thinking Deficits

Higher-order thinking skills are commonly referred to as metacognitive ability or executive functioning skills. They refer to one's ability to reflect critically on academic work or social situations, problem-solve in new situations, see the gestalt or "big picture," and plan steps to complete a complicated project. Students with these deficits have difficulty getting started on projects, proofreading work, completing longer-term assignments, and getting the gist of a reading or lecture. These thinking skills can be taught through specific lessons on "self-talk" (metacognitive strategies), mnemonic strategies, and critical thinking.

No learning-disabled child has all of the deficits above; rather each child has an individual combination of deficits that manifest in various ways.

With these common deficits, it is no wonder that a learning-disabled child has difficulty keeping up with even basic curriculum demands. Take, for example, the skills from a hypothetical fourth-grade curriculum described in the next few paragraphs.

In the area of reading, fourth graders are expected to have very efficient decoding skills and should be applying them to read for speed and accurate comprehension. Common assignments include reading age-appropriate novels; understanding myths, legends and folktales; and giving oral reports on information gleaned from written or oral information. All of these tasks are challenging for a learning-disabled child.

In the area of writing, fourth graders are supposed to have a strong sense of paragraph structure and are writing very fluently in both narrative and expository forms. In fact, many students do basic research about science or social studies. These writing demands can be overwhelming to a student with organizational, language (expressive or receptive), fine motor, and memory deficits.

Accurate spelling also becomes an everyday expectation at this age. Not only are students assumed to have a good visual perceptual system and memory (for remembering what letters and word forms look like), they are also expected to memorize rules and sight words, take oral instruction and dictation, and perform well on tests, quizzes, and proofreading exercises. These tasks are very difficult for a child with language deficits.

Content demands also increase at this early age. In a typical fourth-grade curriculum, students are required to integrate many skills, ranging from the study of animals and plants, to poetry-writing, to dinosaurs and electricity. In mathematics, students must be very fluent in their basic facts, understand graphs and word problems, follow multiple-step problems, compute basic fractions, and understand place value. They are also expected to have a basic understanding of statistics and be able to compute basic calculations and manipulate numbers in their heads. With this high demand for integration and organization, coupled with the language involved in each of these tasks, it is not surprising that learning-disabled students would have difficulty acquiring new information or recalling it later to demonstrate their true ability. Generally, even tasks usually regarded as "fun" become confusing and overwhelming in a short time for these students.

Overall, the typical deficits seen in learning disabled children affect almost every aspect of their academic and social lives. Although teachers and parents often make assumptions about what children should be able to do, they should never make assumptions about the abilities of a learning-disabled child. Instead, parents and professionals involved in the child's life need to answers these questions carefully:

> What gaps does the child have in his or her learning (i.e., what information was never acquired at younger ages)?
>
> What specific language skills need remediation?
>
> How does the learning disability affect the child's life in general?
>
> How can we salvage self-confidence and self-esteem?

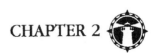

CHAPTER 2

Landmark Teaching Principles

To assist learning-disabled children in the classroom, Landmark School has developed six basic teaching principles that reflect the school's structure and methodology. In sum, they are:

1. Provide opportunities for success.
2. Use a multimodal/multisensory approach.
3. Microunit and structure all tasks.
4. Ensure automatization of skills through practice and review.
5. Provide models.
6. Include the student in the learning process.

Now let's look at these six as they relate specifically to writing.

1. **Provide Opportunities for Success.**

   This is a very important concept. Failure and poor self-esteem often result when teachers challenge students beyond their ability. During written assignments, this occurs when teachers require organizational or elaboration skills that the learning-disabled student does not possess; such situations dash confidence. To avoid this, Landmark begins teaching students at their current level of ability. In doing so, we improve basic skills and build confidence. Later, once students achieve success in more basic writing assignments, they can move on to more challenging ones.

   Beginning writers should practice only basic paragraphs, with little elaboration. Likewise, proofreading and editing requirements should only reflect the basic concepts students have mastered. As students progress, they can be required to apply more advanced concepts slowly—not only increasing the length of the written piece, but also by using more advanced transitional words, elaboration techniques, and proofreading skills. Only with confidence and a solid basic skills base can students make these leaps. That's why it's important to provide opportunities for success.

2. **Use a Multimodal/Multisensory Approach.**

   Multimodal/multisensory teaching is very effective for learning-disabled students. In general, it simply means presenting all information to students via the three sensory modalities: visual, auditory, and tactile. Examples of multimodal teaching during written assignments include:

   visual presentations—including use of the blackboard (for listing ideas, drawing arrows to relate ideas, diagramming, etc.); employing graphic organizing and outlining techniques; using pictures, photographs or videos to generate writing ideas; and creating visual representations (like collages)

   auditory presentations—including conducting thorough discussions before writing (i.e., oral rehearsal); reading examples of good paragraphs aloud; having students read their own writing aloud; and having students take turns leading brainstorming discussions

   tactile presentations—including actual writing of maps, outlines and paragraphs; writing scripts or plays for acting out later; following directions from sequential paragraphs such as how to make a peanut butter and jelly sandwich and how to change a flat tire; and writing descriptive paragraphs about actual objects that students can hold in their hands

An example of a well-integrated multimodal writing assignment is a descriptive paragraph about the beach. You can start off with manipulatives (tactile mode), such as sea shells, sand, and beach grass, etc., and pass them around the room for students to investigate. You can initiate a discussion (auditory mode) simultaneously or after the students have seen and felt the manipulatives. Conversation should focus on:

— students' own experiences at the beach
— activities commonly associated with beach-going (e.g., sunbathing and barbecuing)
— other plants, animals, and objects at the beach
— current problems (such as pollution) affecting the sea shore
— safety hazards associated with the sun or water (such as sunburns and drownings)
— famous beach areas (such as Hawaii, Florida, California, Pebble Beach and Palm Beach)

During the discussion, write students' answers and ideas on the board, as in most brainstorming situations, to provide another visual presentation. Also, show pictures, photographs or videos of beaches, in addition to the manipulatives, to present information visually. Lastly, a field trip to a local beach, although not necessary, would satisfy all three sensory modes: visual, auditory, and tactile.

Overall, a multisensory approach to teaching is not difficult; in fact, many instructors use one already. It is important, though, to be aware of the three sensory modes and to plan for their integration everyday.

3. Microunit and Structure Tasks.

Breaking information down into its smallest units and providing clear guidelines for all assignments are imperative when teaching learning- disabled students. Such microuniting and structuring is referred to as directive teaching. Landmark consistently uses directive teaching. We break every step of the writing process down into its simplest form, with all steps designed to ensure success. Examples for written assignments are teacher-guided brainstorms and discussions, skeleton maps and outlines (with cues provided), structured rough drafting (which often entails copying from an outline or map), and proofreading checklists and acronyms. These activities enable students to proceed in a step-by-step, success-oriented way.

4. Ensure Automatization through Practice and Review.

Repetition and review (spiraling) are critical. Learning-disabled students, in addition to needing high structure and guidance, need a great deal of practice to automatize skills. The Landmark writing process emphasizes practice through consistency. Students always brainstorm, map/outline, draft and proofread in the same way, with constant review of previously learned skills.

5. Provide Models.

This teaching principle is simple yet very important. It simply means providing concrete examples of what you expect your students to do. For example, if you are teaching basic sequential paragraphs, provide students with an example of a good sequential paragraph. Write it yourself or find one in a textbook or magazine. Providing models for students to follow gives them an idea of what the final product should be and helps them see the big picture.

Also, you can model at every step of the writing process. In brainstorming, you begin by doing much of the talking and self-questioning yourself, enabling students to see how it is done. All of the beginning mapping and outlining exercises are, at first, completely teacher-guided and class-generated. Proofreading skills are likewise taught through your modeling and self-questioning skills. Throughout learning disabilities literature, modeling is considered one of the most effective teaching techniques. Plan to do it whenever you introduce a skill.

6. **Include the Student in the Learning Process.**

Some teachers have a tendency to view students as passive receptacles to fill with information. This could not be further from the truth — or from good teaching. Students come to class with their own frames of reference. Their unique experiences and knowledge affect them as learners and writers and must be taken into account. Therefore, during every written exercise, accept student input as much as possible. Justify your assignments, particularly with older students who question the relevance of written exercises; accept their suggestions; solicit ideas for assignments, since assigning topics of interest to students makes your job easier; and give ample time for students to share ideas and read their compositions together. In short, an included student becomes an invested student who is eager to learn.

CHAPTER 3

The Complexity of the Expository Writing Process

Generally, when a teacher gives a basic writing assignment, it is considered to be just that: basic. That is, students are required to read the question (consider the topic), compile some information, then finally explain it all in writing. Simple? Not exactly. An assignment like this is actually a compilation of quite a few smaller, language-based steps. A non-learning-disabled student understands these steps and applies them implicitly. A learning disabled student with language and knowledge gaps does not. Such students need the steps to be spelled out explicitly. Landmark's experience teaching learning-disabled children is that, with enough exposure to and practice with the specific steps, students will eventually learn and apply them independently.

Because of the special learning styles of learning-disabled students, expository writing is a particularly daunting task. Some of the "hidden demands" in an expository assignment that make it especially challenging are described below.

Comprehension Demands

To begin with, students must understand the writing assignment at hand. That is, if the teacher asks the students to "explain four causes of the Civil War," they need to understand not only specific concepts about the Civil War, but also what the word "explain" means. Already, two potentially difficult comprehension tasks are embedded in this assignment.

Of course, students can acquire content (about the Civil War) from proper presentation (pacing, employing study skills and semantic mapping techniques, etc.); these are discussed in later chapters.

The other important piece — ensuring that students understand all the words in the question (for example, "explain") — also requires a directive teaching approach. Again, while many non-learning-disabled students implicitly understand this word, learning-disabled students may be much less sure and unable to focus their answers in an efficient way. Therefore, all key words associated with essay answers or general writing assignments must be directly taught.

Students should have a reference list of these words with their definitions. With accurate definitions and plenty of practice answering questions, learning-disabled children eventually understand the various assignments and produce correct answers.

Below is a list, with definitions, of commonly used question words that learning-disabled students may not understand. The list assumes nothing about what students already know (adapted from Bos and Vaughn 1991):

Key Words for Essay Questions

Apply: Discern the principles or main ideas; discuss how they would apply to the novel situation

Compare: Cite similarities; or, look for both similarities and differences; check with teacher for specific requirements

Contrast: Look for differences (and possibly similarities); stress the differences; check with teacher for specific requirements

Define: Write a clear, concise statement that explains the concept or topic

Diagram: Provide a drawing, like a semantic map or flow chart

Discuss: Be in-depth and analytical in your answer

Explain: Give the definitions, reasons or causes; be logical as you show reasons or causes

Illustrate: Use examples or provide a diagram or map; check with teacher for specific requirements

Interpret: Explain your own judgements; justify them using facts

Justify: Provide logical reasons for your statements or conclusions; use facts to do this

List: Provide a list of items or reasons; briefly explain each one to demonstrate your knowledge

Outline: draft your answer, using only main points and supporting details; perhaps use outline form discussed in this book; check with teacher for specific requirements

Prove: Use facts to support your argument; show a well-developed, logical argument

Relate: Show the relationship or connectedness between/among ideas; use an accompanying diagram if necessary; check with teacher for specific requirements

Review: Write a critical summary which not only highlights main ideas, but also includes your own analysis and opinions

Summarize: Highlight main ideas without providing your own analysis and opinions

Trace: Explain the development, progress or history of something

To use this list effectively, students need to be taught exactly what the words mean, with lots of discussion and clarification. Next, they should complete some practice exercises to demonstrate their understanding.

Study Skills Demands

Since most content writing assignments are based on reading, lecture, or another class experience, students implicitly rely on study skills to acquire information and express what they learned. Study skills are involved in more ways than one might imagine.

More often than not, content teachers rely on textbooks and reading skills to convey information. A typical middle- or high-school assignment often involves reading a chapter (or section), evaluating it, then producing a written assignment. These assignments can vary from "evaluating" to "summarizing" to "explaining causes or effects." Whatever the assignment, the assumption is usually that students are effectively using the textbook to gather information.

Many students have weak textbook skills. They may have no idea how to manage their time to get through a long chapter. They may have difficulty distinguishing main ideas from details and get bogged down in details without understanding the basic theme. They may not know how to highlight information or take notes effectively, which affects their ability to remember basic concepts. They may not understand how graphics or visuals embedded in the chapter relate to the written text. They may not understand how to organize information graphically or produce a semantic map to ensure their own understanding. Last, they may not understand how end-of-the-chapter questions cue them on the important information.

Basically, many skills are hidden within an assignment and require the gleaning of information from a written text. If students are lacking or dysfluent in these skills, they have trouble completing the assignment.

Critical Thinking Demands

By the time students are required to write in an expository manner, teachers usually assume that they have reached some level of abstract reasoning ability. Generally, expository assignments ask students to "evaluate," "explain," discuss "causes," and interpret "contrasts." Although some assignments are more concrete than others, they are usually asking — at some level — for interpretation, extrapolation, or evaluation on the part of the student.

These types of tasks can be exceedingly difficult for students with learning difficulties. Not only do such tasks demand vocabulary and content knowledge, they also demand synthesis of a wide range of information. That is, students are required to glean information and draw connections and conclusions. In addition, the teacher may also want textual support of ideas, which may be difficult for the learning-disabled student to generate or organize.

Overall, common expository assignments at the middle- and high-school levels often make unrealistic assumptions about students' abstract reasoning abilities.

Organizational Demands

Effective expository writing is absolutely dependent on good organizational skills. Appropriate paragraph and multiparagraph structure is necessary. Each paragraph needs a topic sentence, details, and a concluding sentence. Also, details need to be presented in a logical fashion. For essay writing, the demands become even more specific as students try to correlate the structure of the piece with a thesis statement. Overall, students who have difficulty sorting and organizing information have trouble with written assignments.

Text Structure Demands

Text structure refers to the organizational structure of a writing task. For example, the presentation of a sequential paragraph is quite different from that of a cause-and-effect paragraph. In other words, students need to be familiar with the different set-ups and structures of various pieces of writing. Equipped with this knowledge, they can then reproduce the structures themselves and produce clearer writing.

All paragraph text structures, though varying in their presentation of details, have two things in common: they maintain the same basic paragraph structure (a topic sentence, details, and a concluding sentence), and they all have unique transitional words and phrases that enable the paragraph to flow smoothly. When students know appropriate words and structures to write various types of paragraphs, they can tackle almost any writing assignment.

However, learning-disabled students who lack knowledge of paragraph structure and transitional words are not necessarily familiar with particular text structures. As a result, direct instruction is once again necessary to teach these skills. Students need to be shown the appropriate text models and provided with opportunities for practice and review. Over time, students should be able to commit various structures to memory and apply them more independently. Various text structures for paragraph types are discussed in detail later in this book.

Objective Voice Demands

Students inevitably begin their writing experiences in a narrative, personal form. In preschool, kindergarten, and early elementary school, students tell or write stories from personal experience. These are important activities for them, since narratives allow them to practice fluency and sequencing skills. Common activities include show-and-tell, journal writing, and general story writing about vacation, weekend, family, or holiday experiences. Although most children are more fluent in this form, some need extra help learning story grammar — understanding essential elements of a story (for example, setting, plot, characters, conflicts and resolution) — and how they interact to make a story interesting. Nonetheless, narrative writing is generally regarded as an easier task than expository writing due to its personal and creative nature.

Therefore, it is not surprising that many children have a difficult time making the leap from personal writing to a more objective expository form. Expository writing is harder because of the comprehension, study skills, critical thinking, organizational, and structural demands it makes on students. No longer can students rely on the casual form of storytelling; no longer can students freely choose structure and form; no longer is the writing from personal experience. Instead, the writing is much more objective and largely controlled by structures not known by students. For these reasons, exposition presents a challenge.

Oral Rehearsal or Discussion Demands

A very important link exists between discussing a topic and writing about it. Specifically, the more opportunity students have to talk about a subject, the more easily they can write about it. At the younger ages — and particularly in the narrative realm — lots of discussion is incorporated before writing. For example, a teacher of young students almost always begins an activity with anticipatory questions and discussion. If students are about to read a story about a monkey, the teacher asks, "How many of you have seen monkeys at the zoo? on TV? What kinds of things do monkeys do? Have you ever seen a monkey anywhere else? Would you like to have a monkey? What would be good or bad about it? What do you think this monkey will do in this story? Let's look at the pictures to help us."

The point of oral rehearsal is to activate prior knowledge and make connections among bits of information students already know. Later, when students are trying to read or write about the topic, they have greater reserves of knowledge from which to pull; they read, speak, or write from points of strength.

Unfortunately, as students become older, oral rehearsal is increasingly neglected in the writing process. By middle school, students are often simply given writing assignments without benefit of full discussion. Sometimes these assignments involve writing about concepts never discussed in class — or, if they have been, they are only indirectly linked to the discussion. Of course, the teacher's purpose is to increase independence and critical thinking skills; teachers want students to perform well with the least amount of assistance. However, consistent, effective use of oral rehearsal or discussion is not a crutch as some teachers may believe. In fact, it actually teaches students the valuable skill of group work and discussion and how effective group work can clarify concepts for everyone. It also helps students develop critical thinking skills more quickly since they are regularly being shown (through modeling) how to think about a topic and present it in writing.

As useful as discussion is to the writing process, the two are usually not directly linked in the upper grades. As a result, students may read about one topic or event, hear a lecture on another, then write on yet a third idea or concept for homework. As a result, critical linkages are not made among all three topics, and written assignments are not as clear, strong, or analytical as they might be.

Although oral rehearsal is important for any child's writing skills, it is especially important for learning disabled students. Not only does discussion allow for further practice of their weak language areas, it also helps them clarify foggy or disorganized ideas by talking about them first. Last, learning-disabled students greatly benefit from the teacher's or fellow students' added suggestions about their ideas. In short, oral rehearsal adds yet another avenue for learning-disabled students to receive important, necessary feedback about their skills and ideas.

In summary, when assigning expository or content writing, always follow these rules:

—Teach key comprehension words to ensure that students understand the directions or task at hand. Have students learn the key words and their meanings.

—Make sure that students have appropriate study skills. Check for apparent and not-so-apparent study skills required to complete the assignment. Take note whether highlighting, mapping, or textbook use is necessary for the assignment. If so, is each child capable of that? If not, what can you do to remedy the situation and make the assignment success-oriented?

—Take into account students' critical thinking abilities. Can each child, for example, synthesize information in the way required?

—Assist with organizational skills to ensure the most clear presentation of ideas. This includes helping with study skills and outlining.

—Teach specific text structures for learning various paragraph types. Some children may learn these by implication; however, most need some degree of direct instruction to write most clearly.

—Appreciate the leap that students make from personal narrative writing to more abstract, critical, and objective writing. This leap is more difficult for some than others.

—Provide oral rehearsal or discussion before every assignment. Provide good anticipatory questions; activate prior knowledge; draw connections among bits of information; teach students to make predictions. Help them to write from points of strength.

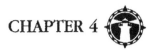

CHAPTER 4

Examples of Expository Writing Across the Curriculum

By the time a child is in late elementary school, expository writing demands are almost everywhere, in every subject. Below are some examples.

—Art class (sequential task): "Explain the four major steps that must be completed before firing your piece of clay."

—Social Studies class (enumerative, descriptive task): "List the three branches of U.S. government and describe their roles."

—Science class (compare/contrast task): "Compare the physical characteristics of a skate and a sting ray. Also, discuss their major structural differences."

—Math class (cause/effect task): "If angle A were decreased by five degrees, explain how triangle ABC would no longer be equilateral. Be sure to mention all other angles and sides."

—Language Arts/Literature (opinion/evaluative task): "Not many people in the book like T.J. What is your opinion of him and how he treats others?"

—Social Studies, Language Arts and similar classes (descriptive task): "Describe the plight of a farm family during the Dust Bowl."

In sum, sequential, enumerative, compare/contrast, cause/effect, opinion, and descriptive tasks are an everyday occurrence in the curriculum from late elementary school to college. Without proper guidance, many learning-disabled students have great difficulty demonstrating their true knowledge.

Expository skills are also important in the development of life and workplace skills. For example, without some basic structures for organizing thoughts, how will a language-disabled person effectively talk about a movie? How will this person have concise, topic-related discussions in social situations? The world is not terribly charitable toward people who talk too much, or who never seem to "get to the point." Strong organizational teaching can help these people both to express themselves better and understand others' explanations.

In the workplace, effective expression and organizational skills are a necessity. For example, school admission and work placement often require application essays. A person needs to be able to explain why they want to study at a particular school or why they are applying for a certain job. Later on, business letters and other basic correspondence skills are necessary. Early on, students need to learn how to write letters of complaint, appreciation, concern, or request as a part of their daily personal and professional lives. Writing work memos (instructional or informative) and reports (summaries, time sequences, interpretations) are often required as well.

Good organizational and expository skill teaching enables students to complete such tasks with more success and confidence.

CHAPTER 5

The Landmark Writing Process

INTRODUCTION

In accordance with Landmark teaching principles, the writing process is taught as a series of manageable steps that can be demonstrated and practiced in very concrete ways. The five-step process itself (brainstorming, organizing, drafting, proofreading, and final drafting) is not unique in and of itself. (See Appendix A on page 47 for a review of various writing methods in the literature.) What is unique to Landmark are the consistency and detail with which these steps are applied.

For each writing assignment—other than a journal or free writing assignment—students are required to follow the five-step process very carefully. In fact, most of a student's grade is determined by whether the steps were properly incorporated. The reason for this is that Landmark wants to reinforce writing as a process that must be continually applied and practiced. Landmark also wants to remind students that writing is never quite finished (for anyone, including teachers) and that further discussion and editing can always strengthen or clarify a piece. Over time, students learn that good writing does not happen in one draft, and that they must be patient to produce their best work.

The basic Landmark writing process addresses those skills and teaching strategies that learning-disabled students commonly need.

Through brainstorming, teachers address the issues of oral rehearsal and immediate feedback on ideas. Emphasis is on group work and discussion, as well as visual organizers to play upon the visual strengths of many students.

Through organizing, teachers convey graphic and visual techniques, as well as outline various text structures before writing. This remediation addresses the organizational deficits so commonly found in learning-disabled students. Students are taught that this step, like all others, is an integral part of the writing process. Significant time is also spent pointing out the similarities and difference among various text structures, and how to write more expansively from a basic outline.

Through drafting, students learn how to address the assignment initially (write a clear and concise topic sentence, experiment with the order of details, etc.) and how to follow an outline correctly. It is here that many students need encouragement and reminders not to expect perfection, but to expand on some basic ideas first expressed in their outlines. Over time, students come to learn (and trust) that they have opportunities later for feedback and revision.

Through proofreading, students learn to apply familiar skills (for example, particular sentence structures or mechanics rules, and vocabulary) and develop metacognitive skills. The proofreading step is an excellent opportunity for students to reflect critically upon what they have written. Critical reflection or thinking skills often need further development in learning-disabled students. With the help of mnemonic devices, checklists, and cueing questions, students can slowly develop these skills.

The final drafting step requires students to incorporate the revisions from the proofreading step. Emphasis is on the actual inclusion of corrections and suggestions; since some students have difficulty seeing how each step is linked, some have trouble actually applying and including final ideas into their final drafts. Some students need special reminders that the reason for proofreading is to improve the final draft. At this step, additional emphasis is placed upon the neatness and overall presentation of the piece.

BRAINSTORMING: OVERVIEW AND SUGGESTIONS

Brainstorming is a very important yet often overlooked part of the writing process. This step provides valuable oral rehearsal of thoughts and ideas, which is essential for learning-disabled students.

Brainstorming offers the teacher an opportunity to help students activate prior knowledge, give feedback on ideas, work together in a group, draw connections among various concepts, and help students develop substrands for topics. Brainstorming also helps develop organizational skills, as students have an opportunity to clarify and organize ideas before they write.

Teachers can conduct brainstorming in a number of ways. The first, and probably most common, is a teacher-led technique. The teacher introduces a topic and solicits ideas from students in a rather random fashion. At the same time, the teacher writes all ideas and suggestions on the board so that students can see what has already been discussed.

Although this may sound like a fairly easy task for the teacher, it actually involves a number of carefully planned steps or techniques. Good brainstorming is not simply allowing the students to talk; rather, it entails careful planning about how to gear a discussion toward specific purposes.

Suggestions for Effective Teacher-Led Brainstorming

First, be sure you have a goal in mind. Know, in advance, where you want the discussion to go to support the writing assignment. Be prepared for what students may discuss and develop ways to draw them in your direction.

Second, accept almost any relevant contribution. The purpose of brainstorming is to activate prior knowledge and creativity, and both vary from student to student. One student may make a connection that you or other students have not made. Therefore, it is important to acknowledge everyone as a valuable contributor, and provide a safe environment for everyone to participate without fear of ridicule. Otherwise, students who feel that their contributions are silly or unimportant will be reluctant to participate in the future and will lose out on the important oral rehearsal experience.

Next, provide cues when necessary. Although brainstorming often sounds like fun to those without language disabilities, it can be daunting to learning-disabled students. Brainstorming involves prior knowledge (which learning-disabled students may not possess), guessing (which can provoke anxiety for students uncomfortable with risk-taking), and some degree of creative thinking. Learning-disabled students often get stuck when they are not provided with enough structure to complete a task. Brainstorming is difficult because of its seeming lack of structure. Some learning-disabled students simply do not like it, and need more parameters than simply, "Give me your thoughts on..."

As a result, cues are often necessary to get learning-disabled students thinking and talking. For example, if a teacher is introducing the concept of the Dust Bowl during the Depression, learning-disabled students may not be able to guess what it is. A typical response from a student might be, "How am I supposed to know? We haven't even learned it yet...." To encourage contributions, the teacher might offer cues like: "How does something become dusty? What do you think of when you think of that word? What about a bowl? What different types of bowls are there? mixing bowls? contest bowls like football? bowl haircuts? What is the shape of a bowl?"

Cues that go beyond the words themselves might include additional information about the topic: "The Dust Bowl refers to an actual place during the Depression. Given what we know about dust and bowls, where do you think this place might be? Why? What do you suppose happened there? Why would we call it this?" Often, cueing questions cause learning-disabled students to realize that they do know a lot about a particular topic; they may simply need more time and discussion to realize it. Over time, the teacher should encourage students to devise and ask their own questions.

When a teacher senses that a student is having trouble with brainstorming, independent brainstorming (i.e., by oneself at the desk or at home) is never a good idea. The teacher should always be available to the student to provide cues and encouragement or supply a willing and supportive peer helper who works well with the student having difficulty.

Another brainstorming suggestion is to expect individual contributions to be on par with the child's ability. It is unrealistic to expect abstract or creative ideas from a child not yet at this level. Instead, closely consider each child's current capability and ask questions appropriate to that level. It may be helpful to think in terms of Bloom's taxonomy, in which you ask questions at a variety of levels to suit each child's needs. By asking each child an appropriate question, you ensure success.

Also, use the board when brainstorming. While students talk, record all relevant contributions on the board. This not only provides visual reminders of what has been said, it also makes it easier to draw connections later between various concepts. Visual reinforcement of information (in which lines are literally drawn between various concepts) is always helpful for learning-disabled students.

Last, set a time limit for class brainstorming. As with any activity, students can become bored if an activity goes on too long. Limit your discussion to a manageable time frame for everyone. A carefully planned discussion should achieve your goals in a reasonable time. Stop when you sense that students are losing interest or when the discussion is not going in the direction you want. Later, you can try again, or when appropriate, move to the organizing step.

Suggestions for More Independent Brainstorming: Acronyms, ISM, and Metacognitive Instruction

Independent brainstorming is a higher-level skill that demands more abstract and critical ability on the part of the student. Most learning-disabled students, when initially learning to brainstorm, need the teacher to lead and cue them effectively. Once the teacher is not present to do this, students are left alone to generate ideas, stay on topic, and develop their own substrands/subtopics. This involves some degree of abstract and critical thinking, which must be developed over time. Without the ability to do such thinking, students may think, "I don't know anything about this. I have nothing to write."

Once you determine that a student can brainstorm without assistance, two methods are helpful: the use of acronyms and a group method called interactive semantic mapping (ISM).

Acronyms
Acronyms, mnemonic devices that cue students' memories for a procedure, can help encourage students to brainstorm more independently. One brainstorming acronym, THINK, comes from the University of Kansas Medical Center (Boyle 1993). It emphasizes the thinking-before-writing-process.

*T*ap:	Tap into what you know about the topic and list at least eight ideas.
*H*ammer:	Hammer away at five good ideas by circling them and linking three details to each (create pods).
*I*dentify:	Identify the pods by linking them together and numbering each one according to where it should occur in the story.
*N*ow:	Now write a paragraph for each pod.
*K*eep:	Keep it neat through a search for spelling and punctuation errors.

Using an acronym does not guarantee improved thinking or brainstorming ability. Rather, the main purpose is to heighten a student's awareness of the brainstorming procedure. Acronyms can also be created by individuals or the class. The idea is to create one accessible enough for students to remember and apply easily.

Interactive Semantic Mapping

Interactive semantic mapping (Scanlon, Duran, Reyes and Gillado 1992) is a more independent, collaborative group brainstorming project. It is highly effective in improving student writing and comprehension. Before reading and writing about new material, the teacher divides the class into groups of five to six students. Each group has a large piece of paper or poster board, plus a pad of Post-It notes. The concept to be studied or brainstormed is written in the middle of the large paper.

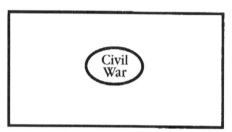

Within each group, one student is the scribe; this person is in charge of writing down all the brainstormed phrases and words. Together, all students brainstorm and make predictions about the concept. As students generate ideas and guess, the scribe writes down every descriptor on a separate Post-It note and sticks it to the paper. Once the students have generated many ideas, the large paper has a messy, haphazard arrangement of note papers.

When the students run out of ideas, they work together to categorize the information. It helps to have a few students pick up a bunch of notes, read them aloud one at a time, and find consensus regarding categories. As major categories are generated, students place notes that fall under the same category together on the big piece of paper. They then draw a line from the center concept out to the category and label that line to make the category clear.

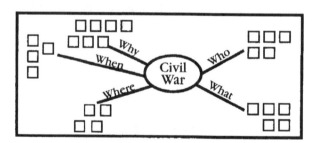

Eventually, students usually categorize all their ideas into four to five major areas. They have constructed a semantic map at this point. This map can be used as an outline for writing or as a comprehension check later.

To use the process as a pre-writing technique, students can write from the map and verify exact facts, if necessary, after they learn more about the topic. Edits can be made during the proofreading and editing process.

Research indicates that ISM can dramatically improve comprehension and quiz scores. Because the students process the information so intently from the beginning, they have increased access to it in memory.

Some helpful hints about ISM follow:

1. Some student groups need help from you while they learn the technique. Although you should try to stay in the background, you may need to give very direct suggestions for categories and keep the students on task.

2. When beginning, you may want to review common categories with the students, so they do not have excessive difficulty with this step. You may want to start by choosing mapping exercises that can draw on the simpler categories such as who, what, where, when, why and how, and remind students of these categories as they brainstorm (if necessary).

3. Especially at the early stages, you may need to remind the students to talk to each other, not to you. At first, students tend to look to you for verification of every idea. Respond by saying, "What does the group think? You should ask each other these questions. Talk to each other."

4. Do not overly use this technique. Although it is generally viewed by students as somewhat fun, ISM takes effort and a positive, cooperative attitude. It should not be used before every writing (or comprehension) exercise; instead, it should be used sparingly to maintain enthusiasm for it. At other times, use regular teacher-led brainstorming or individual brainstorming to serve your purposes.

5. Possibly, assign the role of leader. This person can monitor interruptive behavior, make sure all are heard, and spearhead the categorization process. A leader can further reduce the amount of teacher-led brainstorming and increase interactive brainstorming.

Overall, ISM is valuable because it helps students:

—activate prior knowledge more independently
—tie new knowledge with old
—predict relationships
—use cooperative knowledge
—understand concepts in relation to context
—justify relationships that exist between and among concepts
—confirm their understanding and study for tests and quizzes
—construct semantic maps

Metacognitive Strategies

In traditional metacognitive training, students are taught to ask themselves key questions during the brainstorming process that allow them to be independent and lead them to a finished product. This type of cognitive strategy instruction is commonly used with learning-disabled students, who often lack the ability to self-question and plan effectively. They need direct instruction to do this. Teachers most often teach this skill during long-term projects (for time monitoring and procedural purposes) and for critical writing.

When writing, self-talk is necessary because students must constantly question their writing. The self-questions, "Am I being clear? Am I addressing my audience effectively? Have I answered the question?" are all a part of the writing process. Generally, non-learning-disabled students do this quite naturally without any formal training. However, learning-disabled students sometimes lack the language structures (and, hence, critical thinking skills) to do self-talk on their own. Teachers must teach them these skills in a formal manner.

Researchers have been investigating this aspect of the writing process for learning-disabled students. For example, Englert and Raphael (1988) have developed sets of self-questions to accompany each step of the writing process. They call this cognitive strategy instruction in writing (CSIW). The idea is to develop question-asking in the students to boost metacognitive skills. These skills, in turn, should help their writing.

In the brainstorming step, they suggest questions like:

—Who am I writing for?
—Why am I writing this?
—What do I already know about this topic?
—How can I group my ideas?
—Can I organize them according to a text structure that I know? (for example, comparison/contrast, explanation, problem/solution)

Additional brainstorming questions are:

—What is my topic? Do I know related topics?
—Who is my audience? What is the best way to address them?
—Can I relate this topic to anything I already know?
—Where can I get more information? Who can I ask?
—What is the best way to present this information?

Ideally, students should have sheets with these questions already on them so they can fill in their own answers and cue their thinking. Also, repeated exposure to the same type of questions for all forms of writing helps students learn and internalize the question types.

One key to independent metacognitive skill and brainstorming is correct modeling. You provide questions and initially model their correct use. A second key is repeated exposure to a reliable procedure. Repeated exposure to the sheets with questions helps students to internalize the information and apply it independently. When students use the same questions for an extended time, they begin to learn them on their own and achieve independence.

4. Statement PIE Method

This technique is considered a strategy for paragraph writing, as it generates details for writing (Hanau 1974 as cited in Wallace and Bott 1989). However, in a modified form, it can also be used for brainstorming because it gives direct suggestions for students to think about. PIE stands for:

—**P**roof
—**I**nformation
—**E**xamples

During a brainstorm, an acronym like PIE can help students think in a more direct way about the concept.

Overall, the importance of brainstorming, whether teacher-led, independent, or interactive, cannot be overestimated. Because of the strong link between oral and written language, appropriate rehearsal of thoughts and ideas is imperative to good writing. Without a brainstorming session, learning-disabled students are often at a loss about what or how to write. With a good brainstorming session, they can more confidently and enthusiastically put pencil to paper.

ORGANIZING INFORMATION FOR ROUGH DRAFTING

After brainstorming has been completed, students must organize their thoughts more formally. Sometimes, part of this is done in the brainstorming session. However, learning-disabled students generally need to take organization a step further to demonstrate their best writing. With a more formalized map or outline as an aid, they can better cue themselves for necessary transitional words and sentence structures. As a result, their rough draft — the next step in the writing process — is better.

Two common ways of organizing information for students are graphic organizing (or mapping) and outlining. Mapping was discussed as a brainstorming technique in its common web-like form; however, in more advanced forms, it can help to organize information more formally by illustrating particular text structures (like compare/contrast, enumerative, and cause/effect) in a very visual, effective way.

Outlining is the more traditional form of organizing. The basic paragraph outline that Landmark adheres to is a very simplified format that reinforces topic sentence, details, and clincher; this format repeats among various paragraph types. Using this simplified form, and through repeated exposure, students internalize good paragraph structure and the key transitional words that go with various structures. Outlines for multiparagraph and essay writing are constructed in a fashion similar to paragraphs, using an introductory paragraph (with thesis statement), body, and concluding paragraph instead of topic sentence, details, and clincher.

Both mapping and outlining techniques can work well as organizational tools before writing. Some students prefer one technique over the other, or they use them together to clarify their ideas further. In addition, some students not only prefer one type but need one type more than the other. For example, students who need direct prompting for complete sentences and appropriate transitional words need the more traditional outlining, since this format offers more cues in these areas.

Graphic Organizing

Graphic organizing is simply a visual representation of information. Much has been written about graphic organizing (Englert and Raphael 1988; Black and Black 1990). Vellecorsa, Ledford, and Parnell (1991), for example, use a "hamburger" visual to represent paragraph structure.

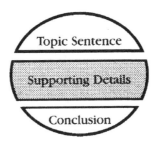

Many learning-disabled students — because of their visual strengths and lack of language fluency — prefer this mode of representation. Graphic organizing reduces language per se and relies on more of a picture to describe relationships. The hamburger example clearly shows that the topic sentence comes first, the details second, and the conclusion last. It also shows that the topic sentence and conclusion surround the details, much like a bun. Last, the details are the meat of the paragraph, the part that gives the most important and specific information. The hamburger conveys all this information to the student with hardly a single word spoken or explained. It offers a concrete explanation of a much more abstract concept.

The hamburger example is very pictorial in nature; it is an actual depiction of a well-known object. However, most graphic organizers rely less on real-life objects and more on diagrams, chains, or maps to depict relationships among concepts and details. Some common graphic forms follow.

Venn diagrams show overlap and separateness. They are useful for writing about similarities and differences, comparisons/contrasts.

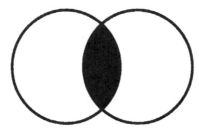

Causal chains or sequential chains show causes and effects, and chronological order.

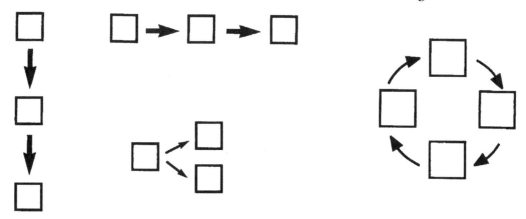

Cognitive or semantic maps show relationships and branches.

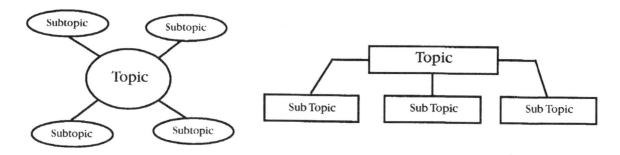

These common forms can be useful in guiding writing because of their visual nature. Often, students who have trouble initially comprehending the structure of a writing assignment can better understand it by using a graphic organizer or text map. See Appendix B on page 53 for examples of graphic organizers.

Outlining for Paragraphs

Outlining emphasizes paragraph structure more than graphic organizing. Some students may actually need the linear strategy of outlining more than graphic organizing because of its clearer emphasis on paragraph structure and transitional word cues. Outlining is a much more formalized approach than graphics, which may in fact be most effective when used in conjunction with outlining strategies.

Outlines are also commonly known as paragraph frames. Paragraph frames are well-founded in the literature. They are not considered cloze procedures (methods that commonly test for comprehension by leaving blanks in sentences that students fill in through their understanding of context clues in the passage). However, frames are similar in that they provide many contextual clues that cue students to provide correct answers. This high degree of structure and cueing makes it almost impossible for students to use the wrong text structure (or paragraph type) when writing.

The philosophy behind frames is simple. While there is a high degree of structure at first, making it easier for students to perform, they actually provide the repetition necessary for the internalization of skills. All the types of paragraphs frames in this book essentially look the same, with only small, detailed differences. Through constant use of essentially the same structures, students slowly internalize correct structures and are ultimately able to produce them on their own.

This strategy of repeating and modeling the correct format is congruent with current learning disabilities research. To remediate lagging language skills, correct modeling and constant repetition of skills are necessary on a regular basis. Although time-consuming, there are significant benefits because of how salient the information becomes in students' minds. A particular challenge in using frames on a consistent basis is fighting the boredom that some students experience during intense remediation. However, creative teaching and varied content information should combat this.

As you study and employ the outlines that follow, please note the repeated emphasis upon:

> —correct paragraph structure (topic sentence, details, clincher)
> —use of correct transitional words
> —use of elaboration techniques (as students become more advanced)
> —requirement and insurance of complete and correct sentence structure

Suggested Methodology for Using Outlines

First, teach students the basics of paragraph structure. Familiarize them with the concepts of topic sentence, details, and clincher or concluding sentence. See Appendix B for basic paragraph structures.

Then, start at the basic level (sequential) and only proceed when adequate practice and a satisfactory level of mastery are achieved. Next, move on to the next type of paragraph in the appendix.

After students master the basic text structures (all the way up to descriptive), proceed to the more advanced forms which involve elaborating on thoughts to make paragraph writing more sophisticated and informative. Elaboration is achieved via the five "W" questions, plus "how": who, what, where, when, why, and how? The most common and easiest one for students to use to expand their thoughts is, the "why?". For example, a student may write:

> *Abe Lincoln never finished high school, but he became an excellent debater and statesman nonetheless.*

An elaborating thought that answers why is:

> *Despite coming from a poor family, he studied independently and read many books.*

In other instances, "what?" or "when?" elaboration is also quite helpful. For example:

> *At Auschwitz, Otto's job was to use his medical expertise against his own will.*

An elaborating thought using the "what?" question (to generate more information about what the job entailed) would be:

> *At the camp, all Jewish doctors were called to perform terrible experiments on fellow prisoners.*

An elaborating thought using the "when?" question is:

> *This was required of him from the day the Nazis found out he was a trained doctor.*

Other elaboration examples that answer the questions "who?", "where?", and "how?" follow, in that order:

> *Otto was an Austrian-trained doctor when he was sent to the death camp.*

> *He was forced to work in the make-shift lab, and prisoners from all over the huge camp were brought to him each day.*

> *The Nazis obtained his cooperation through death threats against him and his family.*

By using these questions, the students expand their language (practice their writing fluency) and add more detail and information to the paragraph. After choosing an elaboration technique, students can move onto the next fact, and likewise elaborate. The finished product is a detailed, cohesive paragraph.

Again, with enough practice elaborating after each fact in the paragraph, students begin to internalize this structure and produce and eventually remember it themselves. Ultimately, they can write a sophisticated paragraph without the cueing of the actual frame or outline. See Appendix C on page 61 for examples of paragraph frames/outlines.

DRAFTING

Students' abilities to draft paragraphs from graphic organizers or outlines vary. You, as the instructor, need to gauge the abilities and progress of your students and teach accordingly. Some students can draft fairly good sentences just from notes in a graphic organizer or outline. Others have a great deal of difficulty working from notes and need a highly structured paragraph frame that force complete sentence structure. With these students, a draft is merely a copying of the outline, except in paragraph form.

Most often, work from highly structured organizers and outlines in the beginning. Then, as students become more fluent and confident in their writing (show good organization, use the proper transitional words, and write in complete sentences), they may write from only notes.

General Suggestions for Drafting Paragraphs

Write in complete sentences during the organizing (during mapping or outlining stages). For students who have difficulty writing in complete sentences, this provides good modeling and prevents them from over-focusing on sentence structure when the main emphasis should be on paragraph structure. With this method, students need only copy the correct sentences from their maps or outlines into their rough drafts.

For students using only notes in their organizing stage, review good sentence structure before they begin to construct their rough drafts. Remind them that every sentence needs a subject (who or what) and a verb (the action or state of being of the subject) and must express a complete thought. Also remind them that subjects and verbs should be embellished with descriptors (adjectives) and additional phrases telling how, when or where the action occurred. How, when and where are often expressed via prepositional phrases. Practice writing embellished sentences in structured exercises.

Be sure that students understand paragraph shape:

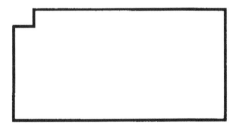

Often, students unfamiliar with formal paragraph writing do not indent the first sentence of a paragraph or otherwise separate paragraphs appropriately. You can develop a model of correct paragraph shape and post it in the classroom or in students' notebooks.

Often, rough drafting from a map is more challenging than from a basic outline, because transitional words and chronological order are often not included in a map. When working from a map, be sure students first number their ideas and perhaps list some helpful transitional words in the margins. In doing this, they can more easily construct a draft with appropriate order and organization and correct transitional words.

Practice elaboration techniques before rough drafting. (Sometimes Landmark outlines cue for good elaboration, instead of assuming students already know how. Also, maps do not typically cue, assuming students automatically do so.) Remember that students can elaborate by adding sentences that explain who, what, where, when, why or how. At the basic levels, elaboration is not necessary; however, once students become familiar with paragraph structure and fairly fluent in writing various paragraph types, they should begin to elaborate on a consistent basis.

Students can do basic multiparagraph writing by simply linking paragraphs together into a composition. Students should outline and draft each paragraph separately.

Essay Writing

Once students master basic paragraph and multiparagraph writing, they should move on to more formal essay writing. A typical format used at Landmark is the five-paragraph model, which includes both an introductory and a concluding paragraph, plus three body paragraphs:

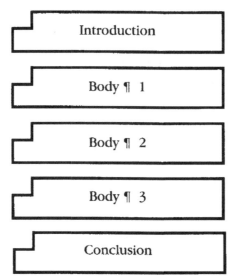

A good way to introduce the concept of an essay is to compare it directly to a paragraph:

In a paragraph:

Topic sentence introduces subject

Detail sentences add specificity and extra information on topic

Concluding sentence wraps up the paragraph

In an essay:

Introductory paragraph introduces subject (contains a thesis statement)

Body, or detail, paragraphs add specificity and extra information on topic

Concluding paragraph wraps up the essay

Once students understand that the structure of the essay is essentially the same as a paragraph, they can begin to practice the essay.

Teaching Essay Writing

The first step in teaching essay writing is to analyze well-written essays. The objectives are to model correct structure and give students practice outlining. Begin by reading a well-structured five-paragraph essay, and filling in a skeleton outline with the students. See Appendix D on page 83 for an example of a skeleton outline.

Next, teach students how to identify and write thesis statements. This is important because a thesis statement serves as a topic sentence for the entire essay. It explains students' position and how they will support it in the composition.

In a general five-paragraph essay, the thesis statement is the last sentence in the first paragraph. It contains three parts (Sullivan 1980):

   —topic: the subject of the essay
   —controlling idea: what the writer is saying about the topic
   —supports (usually three): how the writer will prove the controlling idea

The thesis statement is very important because it not only serves as a topic sentence for the composition, but it guides the outlining of the essay. The three body paragraphs are determined by the three supports in the thesis.

An example of a well-written thesis statement is:

> *Recycling is important because it preserves the environment, saves money, and creates new business.*

The topic of the statement is recycling. The controlling idea is that recycling is important. The three supports are that recycling preserves the environment, saves money, and creates new business.

A good way for students to start identifying and writing thesis statements is to complete various structured exercises. Students should be required to label the topic, controlling idea, and supports in each statement. They can also be required to offer supports to statements that may be missing them.

Once students are familiar with the structure of a thesis statement, challenge them to write some of their own. An easy way to begin is to provide students with interesting topics on which they can take positions. Topics conducive to debate or opinion might be capital punishment, professional sports, gender issues, television, education, politics, drugs or alcohol, health care, careers, crime or law enforcement, and vacation spots.

Once students can develop a good thesis statement, teach them to outline their essay based upon the thesis. The thesis statement guides the outlining of the essay. Specifically, the three supports within a thesis statement determine the contents of the three body paragraphs. Therefore, in the recycling example above, the first body paragraph is about the environment, the second is about saving money, and the third is about creating new business.

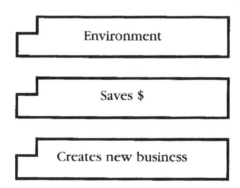

Students can create simple outlines based on their thesis using the framework below.

Thesis statement: _____

_____

1. First body paragraph topic: _____

        a. _____

        b. _____

        c. _____

        d. _____

2. Second body paragraph topic: _____

        a. _____

b. _____

c. _____

d. _____

3. Third body paragraph topic: _____

a. _____

b. _____

c. _____

d. _____

Note that students should not be concentrating on introductory or concluding paragraphs at this point. Because those concepts are often difficult for students, it is generally best for students to first work on the meat of their essay (i.e., the body or detail paragraphs) and save the beginning and ending for later.

To write or outline body paragraphs, students need effective persuasion techniques. Since most essays are critical in nature, they require students to persuade the reader. Fawcett and Sandbery (1988) suggest five basic techniques for persuasion:

—stating facts which support the thesis
—citing authorities who support the thesis
—giving examples which support the thesis
—predicting consequences (positive or negative) for support or non-support of thesis
—answering the opposing viewpoints

See Appendix D on page 85 for more information about persuasion techniques.

After students learn about thesis statements and how they relate to the format of the essay, introduce them to the (often difficult) concepts of introductory and concluding paragraphs. Begin by teaching introductory paragraphs. After discussing the purpose of such a paragraph, introduce the six common methods for writing one (Adams 1982):

—begin with a factual statement
—begin with a theoretical ("what if") question
—begin with a controversial statement
—begin with a quotation
—begin with a striking statistic
—begin with an anecdote

Also, complete practice exercises and paragraph checklists to develop good introductory paragraphs. See Appendix D on pages 86-87 for more information.

Next, begin teaching concluding paragraphs. Again, be sure to discuss the purpose of such a paragraph first. Practice the five common methods for writing concluding paragraphs (Adams 1982). Note that these methods are similar to those used for introductory paragraphs:

—leave the reader with a question to be answered
—use a quotation or anecdote that supports the thesis
—summarize main points for the reader
—draw conclusions about the information presented
—show a need for change, concern or action

Also, complete practice exercises and paragraph checklists to develop good concluding paragraphs. See Appendix D on pages 88–89 for more information.

After you've introduced students to all parts of an essay, they are ready to piece all the paragraphs together to create a unified five-paragraph essay. All future essays should follow this format.

To summarize the steps of five-paragraph essay writing:

1. Develop a thesis statement.

2. Outline and write body paragraphs based on thesis statement supports. Employ appropriate persuasion techniques.

3. Outline and write an introductory paragraph using one or more methods.

4. Outline and write a concluding paragraph using one or more methods.

5. Proofread and recopy paragraphs into one unified five-paragraph essay (final draft).

PROOFREADING

A common problem that teachers face about the writing of their learning-disabled students is its seeming lack of critical reflection, or proofreading.

Teachers often have writing submitted to them in rough form, with numerous spelling, grammatical or organizational problems. Teachers frequently spend hours reading rough drafts and giving suggestions for improvement, only to have the final drafts passed back to them in almost the same condition as the original. Teachers wonder why students don't reread the work to themselves, identify their mistakes, see that a paragraph does not make sense, or incorporate their suggestions.

The answer is actually fairly simple: critical proofreading, or critical thought, relies on a fairly well-developed metacognitive ability which many learning-disabled students lack. Many learning-disabled students lack the evaluative and problem-solving constructs that enable a non-learning-disabled person to identify and fix mistakes. This same lack of metacognitive ability (sometimes referred to as executive functioning) sometimes inhibits students' ability to problem-solve, apply pragmatic or social skills in group situations, or apply recently learned information to independent situations.

To apply information and critically evaluate situations, students must shift from their position of personal involvement to a more objective position in which they can consider all the data they've learned and evaluate whether their performance is appropriate. Because of the complicated language demands involved in this type of process, it is no surprise that students who lack fluent language skills have difficulty.

Some of the numerous ways to teach proofreading skills or more critical reflections are through:

—proofreading checklists
—acronym strategies
—metacognitive skill development
—peer editing

These methods rely heavily on modeling and repeated exposure.

Proofreading Checklists

Proofreading checklists are aids for students to use after rough drafting to ensure that they meet certain requirements or correctly integrate certain language skills. To create a checklist, students or teachers make lists of all the important skills they think should be reflected in compositions.

For example, if students are working on compound and complex sentences in isolated exercises, a proofreading checklist would include those skills to ensure that students begin to incorporate them into their independent writing. Through repeated exposure to the same checklist (for about a month), students begin to incorporate compound and complex sentences in their writing automatically. If it sounds simple, it is; however, success relies heavily on consistent usage. Students use the list daily, whether the assignment be a short class project, a homework assignment, or longer-term essay. In addition, the checklist format should be consistent, even though skills contained in it occasionally change. Learning-disabled students need to rely on familiar formats to use a tool most easily. Therefore, if your students' checklist starts with mechanics skills and ends with stylistic requirements, be sure all subsequent lists follow the same basic format.

Checklists can be used in a number of other ways. Some students prefer to use them while they write. These students like to incorporate all requirements while they write, or at least make attempts to do so. When they finish writing, they should check the list again to be sure they have indeed met all requirements.

Some students prefer to use checklists only after they complete their drafts. For some, freedom from the list enables them to write more fluently or to test themselves on independent application of the skills. After drafts are completed, students use the list to verify or correct their work. This method is the goal for most students, even though they may start off using checklists while they write.

At the beginning stages, students may need to use the checklists in your presence. You can provide any modeling necessary and can give immediate feedback on student performance. At later stages, students can use the checklists more independently.

Checklists are most effective when built-in assurances exist to ensure students are using them. Build in small requirements that prove students are indeed thinking about what they are learning. For example, if you ask for the integration of two compound sentences, require students to underline them. If you want students to use three transitional words, require they be circled. The same goes for commas, adjectives, concluding sentences or whatever you are emphasizing. If students can't underline or circle a requirement, there is a good possibility they have not incorporated it. Those students need to go back and incorporate the requirement more purposefully. Without built-in assurances, students tend to skim through the list, checking requirements off without thinking about them.

See the following page for an example of a proofreading checklist.

Proofreading Checklist Example

Schumaker, Nolan and Deshler 1985; Gudaitis 1994)

Teachers should remember that checklists should only include those skills the class has already studied.

Directions for students: After writing your draft, check your work using the COPS acronym:

_____ **C**apitalization: Please circle all caps.

_____ **O**ral Reading: Read the piece aloud—do this yourself, if necessary. Otherwise, have someone else read it to you.

_____ **P**unctuation: Please circle all your marks.

_____ **S**pelling (phonetic): Can you sound out all words?

Does your essay have:

_____ ten sentences? (count!)

_____ three transitional words (such as: also, in addition, as a result, therefore, after that)? Please underline them.

_____ good paragraph structure? (topic sentence, details, clincher) Put a check mark at the beginning, and at the end of the paragraph if you have these.

_____ one compound and one complex sentence? Please underline.

_____ one sentence with a semi-colon (;)? Please circle the semicolon.

_____ (Remember, you must have complete sentences on both sides of a semicolon.)

Acronyms for Proofreading

Acronyms and other mnemonic techniques help learning-disabled students. As demonstrated in the discussion of brainstorming, acronyms and mnemonic techniques do not necessarily address correct usage of skill; rather, they remind students of what they are aiming at.

The same holds true for using acronyms in proofreading. Remembering an acronym such as COPS (Schumaker, Nolan and Deshler 1985) does not necessarily guarantee that students will no longer make mistakes in capitalization, organization, punctuation, or spelling. Instead, the technique helps them remember important elements to attend to. This awareness alone aids learning-disabled students in their proofreading, since many lack awareness of even its most basic elements.

General suggestions for using acronyms follow:

1. Use the acronym consistently. The idea is to make the acronym automatic in students' minds, something to cue them to know what to do. Repetition and application are key to effectiveness.

2. Keep a poster of acronyms in your classroom. A poster is a constant reminder of the acronym's meaning and usage. Give students copies of the acronym (with meaning) to place in their notebooks, or tape a copy to special work areas.

3. Give a clear message about the acronym's usefulness. Students need to understand why the technique may be useful. Older students in particular may need additional justification for usage. Explain that an acronym technique gives them a heightened level of awareness about what they should address in proofreading. In addition, parents or tutors who work independently with learning-disabled students may need explanation of the techniques.

4. Use the acronym in conjunction with other techniques. A combination of techniques is likely your best tool. One example is COPS plus a checklist requiring additional proofreading. Later, individual proofreading goals can be developed from the students' own portfolios (i.e., individual writing samples).

Some common acronyms students can use for proofreading:

COPS

— **C**apitalization

— **O**verall presentation and organization

— **P**unctuation

— **S**pelling

With this acronym, specific requirements are up to you. For example, capitalization may refer to the beginning of sentences; overall presentation may refer to correct paragraph shape; punctuation may refer to periods and commas; and, spelling may refer to phonetic representations only. In other cases, these requirements can be made much more advanced.

As with other proofreading techniques, require students to prove they have conscientiously used the tool. Ask that they underline all capitals and punctuation marks. Also ask them to identify who helped them to proofread or commented on the organization of the piece (a parent? a peer?). Also ask them to write down a number of words they believe are spelled incorrectly, so you know they have considered their spelling. (This also helps identify which words may need to be looked up in the dictionary.)

WRITER

—**W**rite

—**R**ead

—**I**nterrogate

—**T**ake

—**E**xecute

—**R**ead

This proofreading technique focuses more on general procedure and presentation. Using the COPS and WRITER techniques together is highly effective.

With this acronym, **W**rite means to write a rough draft, preferably on every other line to ensure neatness during proofreading. **R**ead means to read the paper for content, adding or deleting information as necessary. **I**nterrogate means to employ the COPS strategy and make corrections. **T**ake means to take the paper to someone else for feedback. **E**xecute means to recopy the composition for a final draft. Last, the second read means to **R**ead the paper a final time.

Another interesting aspect of the WRITER strategy is that it encourages students to seek help with their writing (the **T**ake step), at least in the form of an independent proofreader. This is a very important skill related to self-advocacy that often needs to be developed in learning-disabled students. In addition to working on grammatical, syntactical, and organizational skills, students need to develop skills to explain their difficulties to others (such as teachers and employers) and seek help when appropriate. Therefore, the WRITER strategy or a modified version can be important to a writer's development.

SCOPE

—**S**pelling

—**C**apitalization

—**O**rder of words

—**P**unctuation

—**E**xpress a complete thought

With this acronym, the **S**pelling, **C**apitalization, and **P**unctuation requirements are developed in the same way as the other acronyms. **O**rder of words refers to the organization of the piece, and whether or not syntax is consistently correct. **E**xpress a complete thought means to ensure that all sentences are complete.

Other acronyms are available for teaching effective proofreading skills. You and your class may even develop your own acronyms to suit your special needs.

Metacognitive Skills

All the techniques mentioned previously develop self-reflective or metacognitive skills. After all, that is what is necessary for proofreading. However, self-reflective or metacognitive skills are useful for much more than proofreading. They enable students to problem-solve in everyday situations. Therefore, emphasize these critical thinking and reflective skills in everything students do. A good place to start is their writing.

A common procedure is to expand student repertoire of self-questioning techniques. Because many learning-disabled students lack self-questioning strategies to analyze their own writing critically, they need direct teaching of questioning strategies. You need to teach students specific self-questioning strategies so they can better analyze work and problem-solve.

Some questions students should learn for proofreading follow:

1. Did I answer the question asked?
2. Did I explain it in a clear manner? Can my (objective) reader understand my main points?
3. Did I use keywords (i.e., transitional words)?
4. What parts should I make clearer?
5. What questions might my reader have for me?
6. Did I use an effective text structure (organization)?
7. Is it interesting?
8. What parts do I like best?
9. What could make it more interesting?
10. Did I use appropriate examples to illustrate my points? (Did I support my viewpoints or facts?)

Again, a repertoire of questions is personal; it depends upon what the student wants to work on and what you see as areas of weakness. You could start by having all students learn a similar set of questions, then have them apply them as they write and proofread. Questions can become more individualized as students develop their own areas of need. Also, these questions can be modified slightly for use by a peer editor.

Suggestions for teaching metacognitive and self-questioning strategies follow:

1. Use self-questions consistently, the same way you use acronyms and checklists. Without repeated exposure, students do not internalize tools enough to achieve independence.

2. Remind students to use self-questions with posters and notebook reminders.

3. Initially, teach questions through modeling. Show students your own thought process and proofreading techniques by leading a class exercise in which students watch you proofread a piece of your own. (Use an overhead projector to display the paragraph to the class.) As you proofread, correct and improve the paragraph by asking the self-questions you would normally ask yourself out loud. Students not only see how the questions work, they will also begin to understand that everyone asks them when proofreading.

Peer Editing

An important part of proofreading is the involvement of another person. Strategies like peer editing develop self-advocacy skills in writers (because they ask for help) and encourage acceptance of constructive criticism.

To benefit learning-disabled students, peer editing entails pairing students with non-learning-disabled peers who are supportive, willing participants. The peer reads the piece and offers feedback according to acronyms, checklists, or self-questions the class is using to teach proofreading.

If your class is comprised solely of learning-disabled students, try to make pairs of students with complementary strengths. Students can still receive valuable feedback even when both of them have some degree of difficulty with proofreading. For example, a student with stronger grammatical skills can offer valuable feedback to a student with a flair for organization or style, and vice versa.

FINAL DRAFTING

Final drafting is the last step in the writing process. It means to recopy or rewrite a piece so that it will reflect its neatest and most accurate form. Although it seems that the most difficult work has been completed in the previous four steps, final drafting presents its own challenges.

First, learning-disabled students who have successfully completed proofreading exercises may still neglect to incorporate changes in their final drafts. This usually occurs because they do not understand the link between the proofreading and final drafting; sometimes, students view the proofreading step as an isolated exercise, and do not understand that the purpose is to apply changes to the final draft. Also, they sometimes incorporate only some of the changes while leaving others out (due to organizational difficulties).

There are a number of way to avoid these situations. The easiest way is to use the proofreading checklist again to be sure that changes have been included in the final draft. Since many students do not want to mark up a final draft by circling punctuation marks or underlining sentences, they could go through the list orally, either with you or a peer. This way, students can better understand the link between proofreading and final drafting, and the importance of working cooperatively with another person. Also, students can check for required items using only a light pencil; after they have verified all elements (and have shown you or a peer), they can erase the marks. These same techniques can be used if acronyms or self-questions were employed in the proofreading process.

Another challenge of final drafting is getting students to put forth their best efforts. Writing tends to be a laborious process, and many students lose interest by the end. This can occur even with assignments that are short and of high interest. To minimize this, teachers might also require an oral component, whereby students read their pieces out loud upon completion. (This only works if students are generally willing to do so.) If students will be reading their work out loud, they are more motivated to make the final piece neat (for easier reading) and complete. In addition, teachers might publish student work at the completion of the assignment. Students who know that copies of their work will be published in a class book will generally want to write neatly and show their best efforts.

Teachers can also assign compositions specifically for audiences outside of the classroom. Examples of such assignments might be letters to the editor of a local newspaper, articles for the school newspaper, or a letter to a senator. Such assignments are motivating for students because they are not being written for the teacher, but for members of the outside community. Because they are writing for a special audience, students are eager to show their best efforts. Such assignments also give them a greater appreciation for the importance of audience.

In addition, students who have used a word processor during the writing process tend to be undaunted by a final draft. Since corrections are easy — and even fun — to make on a computer, students are not discouraged by the prospect of producing another copy. A final benefit of using a computer is that it ensures neatness in both the rough and final drafting stages. Because of the neat appearance of these compositions, students tend to be especially proud of them.

Another suggestion for maintaining motivation would be to require other activities along with the final composition. An example would be assigning art or other visual representations to accompany the writing. Since many learning-disabled students have visual and creative strengths, these projects tend to be very popular. A specific idea would be to require students to design their own book cover (if the composition focuses on literature). In addition, students can create collages which reflect themes in their compositions. Another idea is to have students role-play certain scenarios or characters associated with their written pieces. With imagination, teachers and students can come up with many ideas which make final drafting more stimulating and fun.

Last, remember that application of new language skills is not the only purpose of final drafting. Final compositions also give students a chance to learn about pride in work and presentation. Therefore, give credit for compositions which are submitted in a neat fashion, following the correct format. Students learn that, even when language skills are difficult — and perhaps not incorporated correctly — it is important to take pride in what they do, and to see projects through to conclusion.

CHAPTER 6

Portfolio Assessment

While independent goal-setting is a desirable skill for all students, it is a skill that language-disabled students do not readily learn independently. As with many other skills, these students must be directly taught how to evaluate their performance, set goals, and systematically work to achieve them. One effective way to teach more independent goal-setting is through portfolio assessment, a popular method for assessing student performance and developing more critical thinking in students (Frazier and Paulson 1992; Paulson, Paulson and Meyer 1992; Rief 1992; Wolf 1992).

Used correctly, portfolios serve as clearinghouses for each student's best work, collections of pieces that reflect that person's best efforts. General portfolios contain work from all subject areas and show the variety of work the student generated: writing, exams, poetry, creative stories, drawings, math problems, videotapes of oral presentations, and more. The basic idea behind such collections is that, as students determine the contents of their portfolios, they need to justify why various pieces should be included and determine future goals to improve the work. A portfolio is a collection of work upon which students must critically reflect to develop higher-order thinking and goal-setting skills. The obvious benefits of portfolios make them very valuable for teaching the writing process.

Writing portfolios are effective for two reasons. First, they offer a broad and accurate assessment of a student's capabilities. With conscientious use, a teacher and student can clearly track progress from September to mid-year to June. If writing instruction (and portfolio usage) is effective, you should see an adherence to goals and an improvement in writing over time. Assessment of progress then is no longer based on one isolated test or a series of grammar worksheets, but on actual work the student produces over time.

Second, a strong portfolio places a good deal of responsibility on the student. Although some students need teacher assistance at the beginning (to choose work and develop goals), most end up being fairly independent — and serious —in their use of the portfolios. They begin to improve their abilities to identify good work and be more independent in their goal-setting. In addition, students who actively participate in their own goal-setting perform better in terms of achieving those goals. They are more invested in goals that they have helped determine. They also seem to remember their goals better throughout day-to-day assignments.

Portfolios aid the proofreading process because, day to day, students are more mindful of what essential elements they should foster in their work. During their proofreading process, they are more conscious of incorporating these elements into their final drafts.

A key element of portfolios is that included pieces always reflect some aspect of goal attainment. Otherwise, there is either a lack of directed progress or the goals set are not appropriate for the student and need to be modified or changed completely.

Suggestions for using portfolios and goal-setting procedures in the proofreading process follow:

1. Provide students with a 3-ring binder or folder system in which they will store examples of their best work. These binders or folders will hold the portfolio of work, and they usually remain in the classroom at all times. Students may occasionally want to bring them home, and how this is handled is up to the individual teacher; however, you will want to be careful to make sure that they are not lost.

2. Set aside at least one day each month for students to work on portfolios and goal-setting. All writing from the prior month should be in front of them, so that students can determine which pieces should go into their portfolios. Each piece that is chosen should immediately go into their binder or folder.

2. Use a consistent goal-setting sheet for students to fill out on each portfolio day. After they select their work, they fill out a sheet that:

> —explains what their included work demonstrates—what its purpose was

> —tells why they included the work by answering such questions as, "Why do I like this piece so much?", "What does each piece demonstrate about my talents?", and most importantly, "How do these pieces reflect goal attainment?"

> —evaluates whether goal progress is satisfactory and tells what the student plans for the future in terms of goal attainment. Sometimes students determine that more work is needed in a particular area, or they decide that their goals have been reached and new ones need to be set for the next month.

This sheet goes into the portfolio, along with the work. This is important because it provides students with the opportunity to systematically analyze their work and record their goals and progress.

3. After students determine goals through the portfolio process, have them copy these goals into their everyday notebooks so they are readily available. Especially at the beginning of this process, students need to be reminded of their goals as they write on a day to day basis. Eventually, they internalize goals and become more independently mindful of them during the writing process.

Goals developed from portfolio usage are another type of proofreading checklist. In fact, the list of goals kept in students' notebooks as daily reminders can be used as checklists themselves for each assignment. Another interesting way to increase student investment is to ask students how they should be accountable for their goal attainment. Perhaps students should decide what penalties should be incurred for poor proofreading? Perhaps they can design built-in accountabilities on their goal sheets much like the proofreading checklists with built-in proof of usage.

CHAPTER 7

Cooperative Learning and the Writing Process

Cooperative learning is a popular technique in many classrooms. The Language Arts Department at Landmark has found that writing in a cooperative learning environment can be a very beneficial and motivating tool for our students. It is especially valuable for learning-disabled students because it encourages independence and problem-solving (metacognitive) skills.

Cooperative Learning is a structured, heterogeneous group situation in which students work interdependently to reach a common goal (Johnson, Johnson and Holubec 1994). In a Language Arts class, this goal generally focuses on writing a composition. In a well-designed cooperative learning situation, each student participates equally; the input of each member is necessary for the success of the project. It is important to note, though, that many group learning skills need to be taught. Therefore, cooperative learning also requires active involvement of the teacher who must consistently give constructive feedback and encouragement.

Cooperative learning is valuable because it addresses many skills during one experience. Johnson et. al. (1994) have found that it:

— fosters less dependence on the teacher, and more on each other; this is what every teacher of learning-disabled students strives to achieve.

— fosters workplace and life skills (creativity, problem-solving, self-esteem)

— develops social skills (peer interaction and cooperation, responsibility)

— fosters the direct application of academic skills (students apply previously learned concepts with each other's help, the teacher's role minimizing

— increases productivity by enabling students to produce more specific and voluminous work

— provides numerous models for students by enabling them to learn directly from each other in addition to learning from the instructor

— fosters a more positive perception of the instructor and others in the class

— fosters metacognitive skills, since students actively work together to solve problems

In sum, cooperative learning is good for teaching writing because it fosters independence, metacognition, and creativity.

Structuring a Cooperative Learning Writing Group

First, specify your objectives carefully. Is your purpose to develop academic or social skills? Generally, Language Arts (writing) teachers focus on the academic; however, the extra social benefits of group learning are valuable to students as well.

Justify the project you are assigning to garner support. Cooperative learning works much better when students are enthusiastic and willing. Explain why both writing and social skills are important, and what you expect students to gain by being a part of the group. Be sure the assignment is worthwhile.

Assign a project or composition that can easily be broken into parts or jobs. This is not difficult with a writing assignment. For example, one student could be the brainstorming leader, another the organizer, another the scribe, and others the proofreader, final typist or overall group leader. With writing, the microunited tasks of the five-step process lend themselves well to job assignments.

Limit group size. Five to six students in a group is ideal, but you may find it necessary to begin smaller (two to three students). Your initial and ultimate group numbers depend on the capabilities (both academic and social) of your students. However, do not exceed six students in a group; too large a group does not lend itself to clear job delineation, and control of discussion becomes difficult. Again, think about the steps of the writing process and the skills you want them to apply when thinking of assigning jobs.

Assign roles or jobs to each student. This is worth repeating because of its integral role in cooperative learning. Without clear job delineation for each student, equal participation cannot be guaranteed; without equal participation, cooperative learning is not achieved. Each child must have a clear, interdependent job within the group to reap the benefits of the exercise. Some roles could be:

> —leader/encourager/coordinator
> —brainstormer/idea generator
> —scribe/notetaker
> —proofreader/editor
> —typist/final reader
> —checker — someone who makes sure everyone understands the   group's procedure and purpose
> —reader — if oral presentation is involved

Another option is for each student to complete all five steps of the writing process; the differentiating factor would be in the materials each student uses. For example, in a five-paragraph composition, each student could be responsible for writing one paragraph for the group. At the end, the group can string the paragraphs together to create the essay. Together, they can proofread or edit the piece as a final step.

Overall, no matter what roles are chosen, there should be interdependence within the group.

Do not rotate or change jobs until students are fairly adept with their roles. As with most tasks, learning-disabled students need much practice and exposure to one skill before moving to others. Therefore, changing roles from day to day may be too confusing and prevent confidence from developing within the group. Keep jobs stable for at least a week.

Assign heterogeneous groupings. Whenever possible, group students according to their different strengths and weaknesses. For example, highly creative students (brainstormers) can benefit from their more structured counterparts (organizers) who are better with expression of ideas. If groups are too homogeneous, they get stuck when they reach a task that no one is very good at.

If you have a mainstreamed classroom, this mixing is easy, as you can group learning-disabled students with non-learning-disabled peers. In a solely learning-disabled class, the task may take a little more thought, but it is achievable.

Have both individual and group accountability. As the teacher, you remain responsible for giving feedback, gauging progress, and keeping accountability. By assigning both individual and group daily grades (or another rating system), you can better motivate students.

Group accountability or grading is daily feedback given to the group as a whole. For example, you may decide to give a particular group a B+ for the day. This type of accountability not only shows students how they are working as a group, but serves to motivate those who may not be motivated by their own grades. (Special educators know many students in this situation.) Specifically, a student probably does not want to be identified (or implied) as the "one bringing down the group grade." Therefore, if all students know that their personal efforts help or hinder the entire group, each may be more motivated.

Individual accountability or grading is daily feedback given to each individual. This grade helps reward students who are working especially hard — and can serve as an important motivator, particularly when a group is not working well together. For example, if a group is off to a rocky start, one hard-working and enthusiastic student may be discouraged if he or she is only graded according to the group. The student may feel that hard work has been overlooked or that he or she has been cheated. As a result, the student may give up for the remainder of the project, perceiving that his or her efforts make no difference. Therefore, an individual grade can help this student to maintain motivation; although the group may receive a C- for the day, this student may receive an A for personal effort.

Provide group rewards. At the end of the writing project, you may ultimately want to test students individually to gauge their progress. However, you should also award credit to all group members for performing at a particular level. That is, final group grades are just as important as individual ones.

Give daily feedback to each group. Especially at the beginning, many group skills need to be taught. Therefore, it is very important to explain and target desired behaviors, so students know specifically what to do. Give suggestions for the next day's work. Also, try to have students evaluate themselves each day. A checklist could be a valuable tool (much like a proofreading checklist).

Give positive feedback via suggestions rather than negative feedback. This is especially important in a group situation. Suggestions — rather than corrections — are more effective during group learning. Examples of feedback include "You all did well on the drafting today; however, I think it might have helped if you increased your discussion and asked for everyone's opinion first. Why don't you try that tomorrow?"

Be generous and vocal with praise. Let individual students know — in front of their peers — exactly what they are doing well. This increases self-esteem and confidence within the group (both individually and among all the members) and heightens motivation.

Set time limits for projects. Because of difficulties with time management and estimation, many learning-disabled students initially need limits set. They may need help developing calendars for completing the project. Your modeling in this area not only develops problem-solving skills (as in how to break tasks down), it also promotes effective time management. Again, many skills still need to be taught, despite teachers' more limited involvement during cooperative learning.

Some sample writing lessons that could be incorporated into cooperative learning activities follow:

- essentially, any type of composition (each student can have a separate job or part of the writing process in a shorter assignment; or each child can do the same tasks, but work with different materials, to complete a lengthier essay)

- research projects — again, microunited steps to research lend themselves well to cooperative learning

- lab reports — this could work well in other content-area classes

- special projects, such as writing a newspaper

—debating, with the requirement of written work, or a script for the debate

—story writing, with students writing the story in "round robin" style, or separately by chapters

—literature assignments in which each student reads and writes about a different author or analyzes different aspects of the same author

—short plays or mock trials which could incorporate script-writing

Cooperative learning lends itself very well to teaching writing, problem-solving, and group or social skills. Intermittent use in the curriculum has proven effective. One of the biggest challenges special educators face is developing students' independence and active role in learning. Cooperative learning is one way to achieve this goal.

Some social skills that can be addressed through cooperative learning include working productively with others, listening effectively, respecting others' opinions, giving and accepting constructive criticism, working independently, developing communication skills, and leading in an encouraging manner. While there are others, these are some of the main ones that are almost always addressed in a well-designed cooperative group.

SUMMARY

The purpose of this book has been to share Landmark's writing methodologies for teaching the skill of expository writing. The language deficits exhibited by many learning-disabled students often prevent them from completing common writing assignments, whether they be basic paragraphs or more advanced essays. Common writing problems often include difficulties in language generation, organization of ideas, and critical reflection or proofreading.

To teach expository writing effectively, an instructor must break down each step of the writing process into its smallest components, and provide specific concrete examples of how to complete each step. Throughout this book, we have discussed the numerous methodologies for completing each step of the writing process. Although it may not be possible for you to employ all of the Landmark methods in your classroom or to use them in exactly the same way, you can adapt them for your own use.

However you choose to use these methodologies, it is important to follow the five step writing process consistently:

- —brainstorm
- —organize (map or outline)
- —rough draft
- —proofread
- —final draft

These five steps help learning-disabled students to tackle writing assignments more systematically and prevent them from feeling overwhelmed. Most importantly, the process approach can be applied in any writing situation. Once students can fluently complete each step, each assignment becomes accessible.

Also, it is important that each step of the process be practiced frequently and in the same manner each time. Consistent practice is the key to making the entire process automatic in the student's mind. After certain skills are mastered, students can move to more challenging levels. Specifically, students should start out with more basic paragraph outlines (with cues for transitional words and no requirements for elaboration); later, they should move to more advanced types in which they must apply more of what they've learned.

It is also important to be mindful of those teaching principles that have proven to be successful with learning disabled students. In sum, they are to:

- —provide opportunities for success
- —use a multi-modal approach
- —micro-unit and structure tasks
- —insure automatization through practice and review
- —provide models
- —include the student in the learning process

Consistent integration of these principles into your daily teaching offers the best possible learning opportunities for your students.

In addition, students can complete writing assignments individually or in cooperative learning situations. In the latter, many problem-solving and social skills can be addressed in addition to the writing skills. An effective method is to vary the requirements of your writing assignments, so that some are completely individual, while others are completed in groups. Finally, the most accurate assessment of writing progress is probably attained through the use of portfolios. These collections of work reflect the best compositions of each student and offer a view of writing ability over time. Ideally, the instructor should be able to view progress concretely as the portfolio develops.

Remember to assess your own methodology and the progress of your students constantly. When necessary, modify the suggestions in this book to meet your own needs.

APPENDIX A:
A REVIEW OF VARIOUS
WRITING METHODS

A Review of Various Writing Methods

Educational literature describes various methods of teaching expository writing. Although some do not provide the structure and microuniting necessary for language-disabled students, others have been adapted and applied to the Landmark curriculum very effectively. This chapter offers an overview of some writing approaches that have appeared in the literature. The purpose of sharing them is to share the basis of some of Landmark's ideas and to give you the opportunity to adapt them to your students' needs.

Paragraph Strategy

With the paragraph strategy (Moran, Schumaker & Vetter 1981, as cited in Stoddard 1987), students memorize the steps below and practice on various paragraph types (enumerative, sequential, and compare/contrast). Research indicates that students improved their writing of all three paragraph types.

    1. Write a topic sentence.
    2. Write at least three details.
    3. Write a clincher sentence.

Example: 1. Topic Sentence: _____

           2. Three Details:

                1. _____

                2. _____

                3. _____

           3. Clincher: _____

Three-Step Model

The three-step method (Vellecorsa, Ledford and Parnell 1991) is based upon the process/conferencing approach to writing. It emphasizes teacher modeling and self-talk/metacognition at each stage. The three stages are described below.

1. In the planning step, students focus on thinking, organizing and discussing. Students should consider their audience and the purpose of their writing. They should do very little writing . Ideas should be in brief form (words, phrases) for later development. Initially, planning is done as a group, with the teacher modeling self-talk and questioning strategies.

2. In the drafting step, students take a first pass at composing. Emphasis is on initial development rather than technical aspects like grammar and spelling. The teacher should encourage students to elaborate on points from the planning stage. The teacher should also model this procedure a number of times (on an overhead) to demonstrate self-talk (for example, "I'm not sure that's the best way to word it, but I won't worry about that now...I'll get that at the revision stage"). Students should move from creating group drafts to individual drafts.

3. The third step is evaluation and revision. The teacher models a particular method — such as COPS (capitalization, organization, punctuation, and spelling), checklists, and key word searches — gradually shifting responsibility to students. Note that reading aloud is an important means of judging the quality of writing.

Statement PIE

In a Statement PIE (Hanau 1974 as cited in Wallace and Bott 1989), students use the acronym PIE to help them generate details for paragraph writing. After writing a topic sentence (statement), students supply proof, information, or examples to back it up.

In this strategy, students utilize an acronym (PIE) to assist them in generating details for paragraph writing. After writing a topic sentence (Statement), students supply Proof, Information and/or Examples to back it up.

Statement: _____

Details:

    -Proof _____

    -Information _____

    -Example _____

Paragraph Frames

Paragraph frames (Nichols 1980) provide students with incomplete frames of paragraphs to fill in with correct information. This is a quick, easy method for students to complete secondary written assignments; however, emphasis is not on metacognitive skill. Common types of frames include summary, time order, and compare/contrast.

Example: Character Analysis

In the story _____ by _____, the major character is _____, who is _____. Another main character is _____. The problem which the main character faces is that _____. The problem is finally resolved when _____. The story ends with _____. The lesson I learned from reading this story was that _____.

Cognitive Strategy Instruction in Writing

The Cognitive Strategy Instruction in Writing (CSIW) (Englert and Raphael 1988) focuses on task-specific strategies (for example, brainstorming during planning, considering audience and purpose, grouping related ideas and determining appropriate text structure) and metacognitive strategy instruction. It has two major components, as follows:

1. **Teacher modeling:** With a writing sample on an overhead projector, the teacher models and rehearses comprehension strategies and elaborates on text ideas through questions, such as "I wonder what the writer meant by that?".

2. **Think sheets:** These sheets prompt students to free them from trying to remember each of the self-questions and strategies for each writing step. The five thinking sheets are:

   —PLAN sheet: "Who am I writing for? Why am I writing this? What do I already know? How can I group my ideas?"

   —ORGANIZE sheet: "What's being explained? Compared? What are the steps? What does the reader need?"

   —SELF-EDIT sheet: Students read a composition, starring (*) the parts they like and questioning (?) the parts they find vague. They then answer questions like, "Did I tell what was being explained? Did I tell what materials were needed? Did I make the steps clear?"These questions match those on the ORGANIZE sheet.

—EDITOR sheet: The peer EDITOR sheet has the same questions as the SELF-EDIT sheet. The same evaluative process is employed and discussed. Later, the writer makes revisions to incorporate suggestions.

—REVISION sheet: The writer considers the feedback given by the editor, self questions, and decides how to implement suggestion.

This method emphasizes teacher modeling, student rehearsal, interactive dialogue, gradual internalization (of the thinking process), peer coaching/cooperative learning and quality thinking.

Essay Planning and Writing Strategy

The PLANS procedure (Graham, Macarthur, Schwartz and Page-Voth 1992) involves means-ends analysis. Students set product goals for what a paper should accomplish and contain, then further articulate process goals for how to accomplish the goals. The steps involve generating goals, developing notes, organizing notes, writing and continuing to plan, and evaluating success in obtaining the goals. This strategy emphasizes problem-solving, a critical component of effective writing.

1. Implement PLANS:

    Pick goals (for purpose, structure, and fluency/length)

    List ways to meet goals

    And make

    Notes

    Sequence notes

2. Write and say more.

3. Test goals.

Using this strategy, students improved in their ability to include basic components of an essay, increase the length of their papers, and provide convincing evidence. Research focused on the argument essay, but this procedure can be generalized to other types.

Text Mapping and Graphic Organizing

A map or graphic organizer (Englert and Mariage 1991) provides a visual representation of students' main ideas and subordinating relationships. Within these structures, students are cued with questions and key words (for example, alike, different than, in contrast to, and similar to). This method helps writers to "chunk" information and avoid collections of unrelated ideas. See Appendix B on page 53 for examples of graphic organizing.

DEFENDS

DEFENDS (Ellis and Lenz 1987) is a strategy for writing and defending a position (a common high-school assignment). This is appropriate for essay-level writing and emphasizes metacognitive awareness.

Decide on an exact position

Examine reasons for that position

Form a list of points that explain each reason

Expose the position in first sentence

Note each reason and its supporting points

Drive home the position in the last sentence

SEARCH for errors and correct

> **S**ee if it makes sense
>
> **E**ject incomplete sentences
>
> **A**sk if it is convincing
>
> **R**eveal COPS errors and correct
>
> **C**opy over neatly
>
> **H**ave a last look

Specific Editing Strategies

Editing strategies often appear in the form of acronyms. The purpose of these acronyms is to help students remember what they should be editing for. Common examples of editing acronyms are:

COPS (Schumaker, Nolan and Deshler 1985)

> **C**apitalization
>
> **O**verall organization
>
> **P**unctuation
>
> **S**pelling

WRITER (Schumaker, Nolan and Deshler 1985)

> **W**rite on every other line
>
> **R**ead paper for content
>
> **I**nterrogate yourself (COPS)
>
> **T**ake paper to someone for help
>
> **E**xecute a final copy
>
> **R**ead again

SCOPE (Bos and Vaughn 1991)

> **S**pelling
>
> **C**apitalization
>
> **O**rder of words
>
> **P**unctuation
>
> **E**xpress a complete thought

APPENDIX B:
GRAPHIC ORGANIZERS

Sequential and Chronological Maps

Sequential and chronological maps are used to help students organize information over time, or explain a process. They often deal with years, eras, periods, steps or stages.

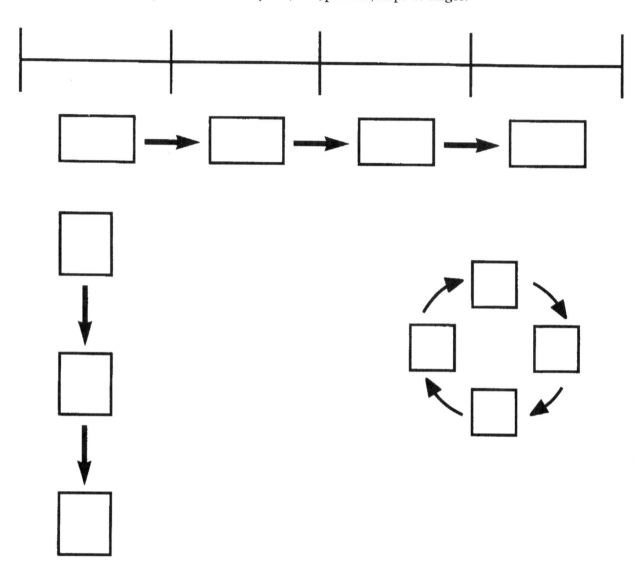

MAIN IDEA 1	MAIN IDEA 2	MAIN IDEA 3	MAIN IDEA 4
details	details	details	details

Enumerative Maps

Enumerative maps help students list or explain reasons, types, kinds, or categories.

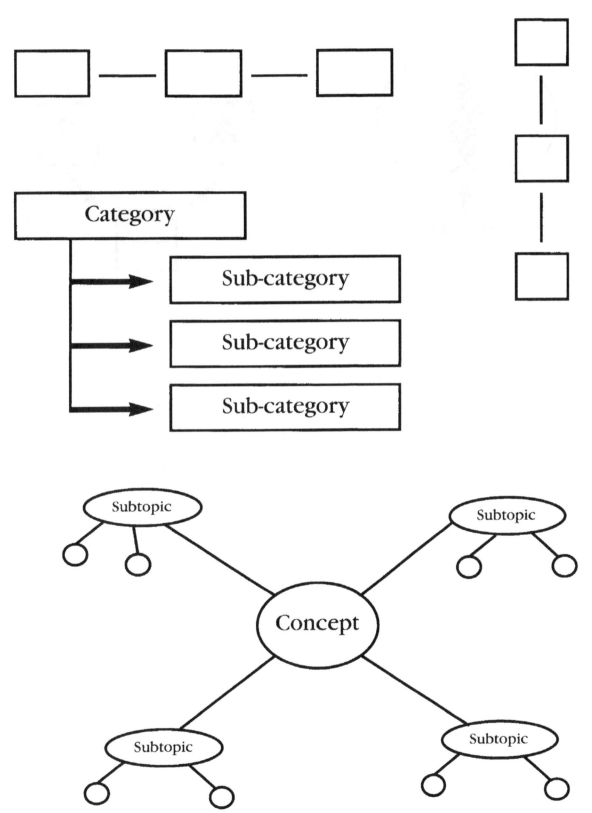

Compare and Contrast Maps

Compare and contrast maps help students to discover similarities and differences. They highlight specific areas or attributes to be examined.

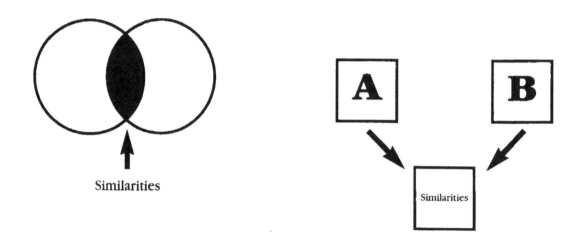

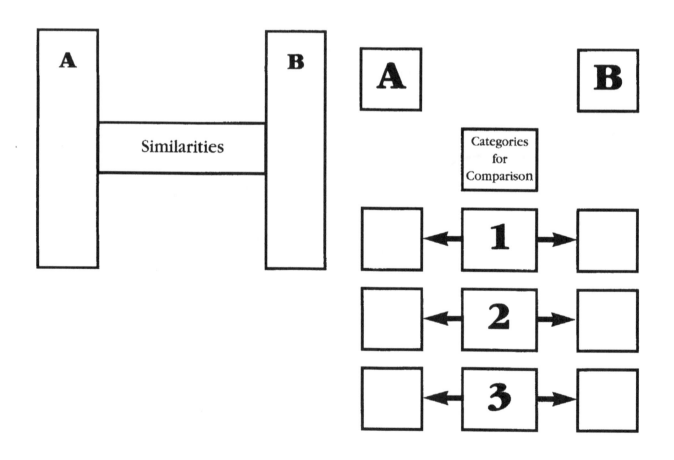

Cause and Effect Maps

Cause and effect maps may indicate more than one cause, or more than one effect. These compositions often use words like "result," "because," and "therefore."

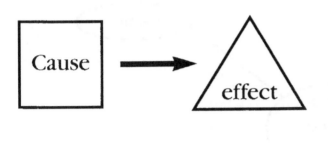

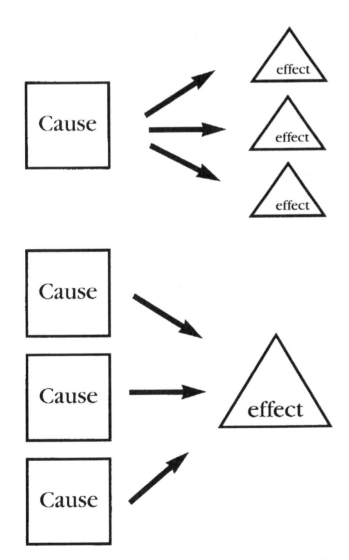

Descriptive Maps

Descriptive maps list or describe characteristics and attributes.

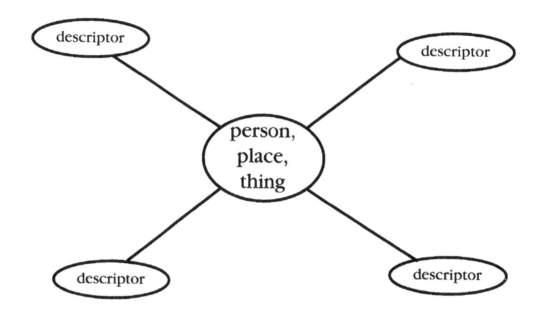

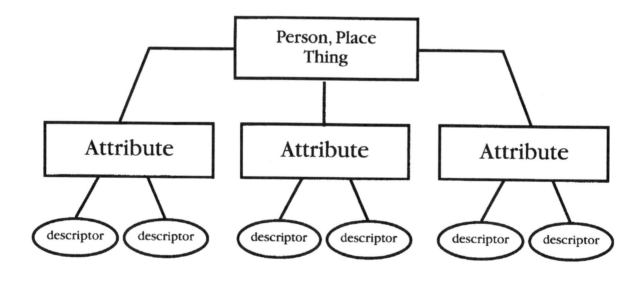

Other Maps

Matrix
(Shows interaction between 2 things)

Concept **2**

Concept **1**

Concept 1 / Concept 2 grid

Arch

Topic

Supports

Main Idea

APPENDIX C:
PARAGRAPHS

Paragraph Basics

The topic sentence should answer a question, introduce a topic, or define a topic. For example, if the assignment is to describe a significant event in the development of U.S. and Soviet relations, then an effective topic sentence might be:

The Cuban missile crisis was a significant event in the development of U.S. and Soviet relations. (answers question)

During the Cuban missile crisis, the world was on the brink of nuclear war. (introduces topic/gives information)

The Cuban missile crisis refers to the time when President Kennedy discovered Soviet weapons on Cuban soil. (defines topic)

Details should support the topic sentence. They differ from paragraph to paragraph, depending on the text structure necessary.

The clincher or concluding sentence is a restatement of the topic sentence, an opinion or general impression, or a prediction. For example:

The Cuban missile crisis was one of the most tension-filled periods in our history. (restatement)

President Kennedy should be admired for his handling of the situation. (opinion)

The Cuban missile crisis will long be remembered as one of the world's most dangerous show downs. (prediction)

Sequential or Process Paragraph

A sequential or process paragraph shows chronological steps or explains a process.

Question or assignment: _____

Topic sentence:_____

_____

Details:

    First step (first):_____

    Second step (then, second):_____

    Third step (next, third): _____

    Fourth step (after that, fourth): _____

    Fifth step (finally, last, fifth): _____

Clincher sentence: _____

_____

More Advanced Sequential Paragraph

This outline for sequential paragraphs is slightly more advanced because it requires elaboration; students need to expand their thoughts on who, what, where, when, why, or how.

Question or assignment: _____

Topic sentence: _____

_____

Details:

    First step (first): _____

    Elaborate: _____

    Second step (next, following this, second): _____

    Elaborate: _____

    Third step (after, then, third): _____

    Elaborate: _____

    Fourth step (finally, last, the end of): _____

    Elaborate: _____

Clincher sentence: _____

_____

Advanced Sequential Paragraph

This outline for a sequential paragraph requires elaboration and transitional words (without cues). You can provide students with word lists if necessary and remind them to elaborate by questioning who, what, where, when, why, or how.

Question or assignment: _____

Topic Sentence: _____

_____

Details:

1. _____

_____

Elaborate: _____

_____

2. _____

_____

Elaborate: _____

_____

3. _____

_____

Elaborate: _____

_____

Clincher sentence: _____

_____

Basic Enumerative Paragraph

A basic enumerative paragraph lists or explains something.

Question or assignment: _____

Topic sentence:_____

_____

Details:

First point/example: _____

_____

Second point/example (also): _____

_____

Third point/example (furthermore):_____

_____

Fourth point/example (in addition): _____

_____

Fifth point/example (finally, last): _____

_____

Clincher sentence: _____

_____

More Advanced Enumerative Paragraph

This enumerative paragraph outline requires elaboration and transitional words (without cues). You can provide students with words lists if necessary and remind them to elaborate by questioning who, what, where, when, why, or how.

Question or assignment: _____

Topic sentence:_____

_____

Details:

    First point/example: _____

    _____

    Elaborate: _____

    _____

    Second point/example: _____

    _____

    Elaborate: _____

    _____

    Third point/example: _____

    _____

    Elaborate: _____

    _____

Clincher: _____

_____

Advanced Enumerative Paragraph

This outline for an enumerative paragraph requires elaboration and transitional words (without cues). You can provide students with words lists if necessary and remind them to elaborate by questioning who, what, where, when, why, or how.

Question or assignment: _____

Topic sentence:_____

_____

Details:

    1. _____

    _____

    Elaborate: _____

    _____

    2. _____

    _____

    Elaborate: _____

    _____

    3. _____

    _____

    Elaborate: _____

    _____

Clincher sentence: _____

_____

Basic Comparison Paragraph

A basic comparison paragraph highlights the similarities between people, objects, events, and the like.

Question or assignment: _____

Topic Sentence: _____

_____

Details:

One similarity is that_____

_____

Also, they both_____

_____

_____

In addition, both _____

_____

A final similarity is that_____

_____

Clincher sentence: _____

_____

Advanced Comparison Paragraph

This comparison paragraph outline requires elaboration and transitional words (without cues). You can provide students with words lists if necessary and remind them to elaborate by questioning who, what, where, when, why, or how.

Question or assignment: _____

Topic sentence: _____

_____

Details:

    1. _____

       _____

       Elaborate: _____

       _____

    2. _____

       _____

       Elaborate: _____

       _____

    3. _____

       _____

       _____

       Elaborate: _____

       _____

Clincher: _____

_____

Basic Contrast Paragraph

A basic contrast paragraph highlights the differences between people, objects, and events.

Question or assignment: _____

Topic Sentence: _____

_____

Details:

First of all, (person/object 1) _____

_____

On the other hand, (person/object 2) _____

_____

Secondly, (person/object 1) _____

_____

However, (person/object 2) _____

_____

Finally, (person/object 1) _____

_____

In contrast, (person/object 2) _____

_____

Clincher sentence: _____

_____

Advanced Contrast Paragraph

This contrast paragraph outline requires sentence combining, elaboration, and transitional words (without cues). You can provide students with words lists if necessary and remind them to elaborate by questioning who, what, where, when, why, or how.

Question or assignment: _____

Topic sentence: _____

_____

Details:

    Person/object 1: _____

    Person/object 2: _____

    Elaborate: _____

_____

    Person/object 1: _____

    Person/object 2: _____

    Elaborate: _____

_____

    Person/object 1: _____

    Person/object 2: _____

    Elaborate: _____

_____

Clincher sentence: _____

_____

Basic Cause Paragraph

This outline for a basic cause paragraph lists causes or reasons for something.

Question or assignment: _____

Topic Sentence: _____

_____

Details:

    The first reason that (or cause of)_____

_____

    Another reason that (or cause of) _____

_____

    In addition, _____

_____

    A final reason that (or cause of) _____

_____

Clincher sentence: _____

_____

More Advanced Cause Paragraph

This outline for a cause paragraph requires elaboration. You can remind students to elaborate by questioning who, what, where, when, why, or how.

Question or assignment: _____

Topic sentence: _____

_____

Details:

The first reason that (or cause of) _____

Elaborate: _____

Another reason that (or cause of) _____

Elaborate: _____

In addition, _____

Elaborate: _____

A final reason (or cause of) _____

Elaborate: _____

Clincher sentence: _____

_____

Basic Effect Paragraph

This effect paragraph outline lists the effects of something.

Question or assignment: _____

Topic sentence: _____

_____

Details:

One effect of _____

_____

Another result is _____

_____

In addition, _____

_____

A final effect of _____

_____

Clincher sentence: _____

_____

More Advanced Effect Paragraph

This outline for an effect paragraph requires elaboration. You can remind students to elaborate by questioning who, what, where, when, why, or how.

Question or assignment: _____

Topic sentence: _____

_____

Details:

One effect of _____

Elaborate: _____

Another result is _____

Elaborate: _____

In addition, _____

Elaborate: _____

A final effect of _____

Elaborate: _____

Clincher sentence: _____

_____

Basic Opinion or Persuasive Paragraph

This paragraph explains or justifies beliefs. The topic sentence should clearly state the opinion, and the details should be facts which support it.

Question or assignment: _____

Topic sentence:_____

_____

Details:

First, _____

Another reason _____

Furthermore, _____

Last/Finally, _____

Clincher sentence: _____

_____

Advanced Opinion or Persuasive Paragraph

This opinion or persuasive paragraph outline is advanced because it requires specific methods of persuasion. Again, the topic sentence should clearly state the opinion, and the details should be facts which support it.

Question or assignment: _____

Topic sentence: _____

_____

Details:

    State a fact: _____

    Elaborate: _____

    Refer to higher authority: _____

    Elaborate: _____

    Answer the opposition: _____

    Elaborate: _____

    Predict a consequence: _____

    Elaborate: _____

Clincher sentence: _____

Advanced Opinion or Persuasive Paragraph

This opinion or persuasive paragraph outline is advanced because it requires specific methods of persuasion. Again, the topic sentence should clearly state the opinion, and the details should be facts which support it.

Question or assignment: _____

Topic sentence: _____

_____

Details:

    State a fact: _____

    Elaborate: _____

    Refer to higher authority: _____

    Elaborate: _____

    Answer the opposition: _____

    Elaborate: _____

    Predict a consequence: _____

    Elaborate: _____

Clincher sentence: _____

Basic Physical Description Paragraph

This paragraph can be used for people, places, or objects. The topic sentence should give a general impression of whatever is being described. In the details section, students should describe sights, sounds, textures, feelings/emotions, and where appropriate, smells and tastes. Each sentences should contain at least two adjectives. Two examples:

> *Eliza's silky, shoulder-length hair was tousled in the breeze.*

> *Eliza's silky hair was tousled in the warm breeze.*

A more advanced paragraph can be written by adding elaboration requirements in the details section.

Question or assignment: _____

Topic sentence: _____

_____

Details:

    1. (sight) _____

    2. (sound) _____

    3. (texture) _____

    4. (emotion) _____

    5. (taste, smell) _____

III. Clincher: _____

_____

Basic Personality Description Paragraph

This outline is useful for analyzing characters in literature. Students are required to use adjectives to describe personality, then cite evidence in the text.

Question or assignment: _____

Topic sentence:_____

_____

Details:

     Adjective: _____

     Evidence/example from text:_____

     Adjective: _____

     Evidence/example from text:_____

     Adjective: _____

     Evidence/example from text:_____

Clincher sentence: _____

APPENDIX D:
ESSAY WRITING

Skeleton Outline Example

Introduction

    Thesis statement _____

Body

    Topic sentence 1 _____

        Supporting detail_____

        Supporting detail_____

        Supporting detail_____

    Topic sentence 2 _____

        Supporting detail_____

        Supporting detail_____

        Supporting detail_____

    Topic sentence 3 _____

        Supporting detail_____

        Supporting detail_____

        Supporting detail_____

Conclusion

    Clincher sentence _____

Persuasion Techniques

Often, a critical essay will require that students persuade the reader. There are five basic techniques for doing this (Fawcett and Sandbery 1988):

Stating Facts

Facts are statements that are true. While they are often statistics or numbers, they are certainly not limited to these. Facts are strong support for an argument or opinion. For example:

> *Forty-two percent of the students believe that...*

Citing an Authority

It is often effective to quote or refer to someone who has known credentials in the field being discussed. The authority should be an expert in that specific field. For example:

> *The Secretary of Education says that an extended school year would be of little use to the average student.*

Giving Examples

Examples can be interesting anecdotes about people or events the writer knows about. The stories should be true and relative to the subject. For example:

> *My friend, John, did well in school because...*

Predicting the Consequences

This technique predicts what will happen if _____. The consequences may be positive or negative. This method often employs such words as "if" and "therefore." It often refers to a time in the future.

> *If the school institutes a mandatory study hall, the students will ultimately resent it and do worse than ever before.*

Answering the Opposition

A good persuader predicts what the opposition will say and answers that argument. This technique requires the writer to provide an answer to the opposition, not just a synopsis of that argument. For example:

> *Some people might say that changing our school curriculum is dangerous, but it would actually improve our program by addressing the changing needs of today's students.*

Introductory Paragraph Examples

The purposes of an introductory paragraph are to:

-state the purpose of the composition clearly

-create interest for the reader

-give information necessary to understanding the topic

Effective methods for writing an introductory paragraph (Adams, 1982) are to begin with:

-a factual statement, such as

"Cigarette smoking has been proven to be a leading cause of cancer."

-a theoretical ("what-if") question, such as

"Is a college education really necessary?"

-a controversial statement, such as

"Prayer should/should not be allowed in public schools."

-a quotation, such as

"Man is the only animal that blushes. Or needs to." (Mark Twain)

-a striking statistic, such as

"The average salary of a recent college graduate is about $23,000."

-an anecdote (a very short, quick story), such as

"The other day I was chaperoning my son's class field trip to the zoo. What I thought would be a relaxing, enjoyable experience turned into a harrowing one. I never knew what havoc twenty-six first graders could wreak!"

Introductory Paragraph Checklist

An introductory paragraph checklist can be useful in helping students to proofread and improve

their work (Crossman 1994). It can be used during or after the rough drafting stage.

Target audience: _____

Thesis: _____

Method(s) of introduction: _____

_____

1. Did the introduction **arouse the interest** of your reader?

2. Does the introduction direct the reader's attention **from a broad, general idea to a**

   specific thesis?

3. Does the introduction act as a **funnel** to limit the topic and focus the controlling idea?

4. Does the introduction establish the **desired relationship** between writer and audience?

Concluding Paragraph Techniques

There are five methods for writing a concluding paragraph (Adams 1982). A student can:

-leave the reader with a question to answer; for example:

> *What will happen to civilized society if we don't do anything about crime? The*
>
> *answer is up to us.*

-use a quote or anecdote that supports the viewpoint of the essay. For example:

> *As Churchill once said, "We have nothing to fear, but fear itself."*

-summarize the main points for the reader; for example:

> *In sum, crime reduction will largely depend upon demographic changes, drug/*
>
> *alcohol education, and new law enforcement techniques.*

-draw conclusions about what has been said; for example:

> *Because crime is so rampant, the likelihood that our children will be victims as*
>
> *some point is very high.*

-show a need for change, concern or action regarding the topic; for example:

> *American citizens need to let their elected officials know that they are fed up with*
>
> *crime.*

Concluding Paragraph Checklist

A concluding paragraph checklist can be useful in helping students to proofread and improve upon their work (Crossman 1994). It can be used during or after the rough drafting stage.

Method(s) of conclusion:

_____

_____

1. Does the conclusion focus the reader's attention on the **central idea (thesis)**?

2. Does the conclusion **summarize** the main arguments?

3. Does the conclusion **invert the funnel** structure of the introduction? Does it move from definite conclusions to their broader implications (i.e., **from specific to general**)?

4. Does the conclusion remind the reader **why the topic is important**?

5. Does the conclusion **maintain a tone consistent** with the rest of the essay?

REFERENCES

Adams, W.R. 1982. *Think, Read, React, Plan, Write.* 3d ed. New York: Holt, Rinehart, Winston.

Black, H., and S. Black. 1990. *Organizing Thinking: Graphic Organizers.* Vol. 2. Pacific Grove: Critical Thinking Press and Software.

Bos, C., and S. Vaughn. 1991. *Strategies for Teaching Students with Learning & Behavior Problems.* Needham Heights: Allyn & Bacon.

Boyle, J. Visual Organizers. 1993. Paper read at session F44 of the Learning Disabilities Association International Conference, San Francisco.

Crossman, S. J. 1994. Introductory and concluding paragraph checklists. Prides Crossing: Landmark School.

Ellis, E., and B.K. Lenz. 1987. A component analysis of effective learning strategies for l.d. students. *Learning Disabilities Focus* 2 (2): 94-107.

Englert, C.S., and T. Mariage. 1991. Shared understandings: Structuring the writing experience through dialogue. *Journal of Learning Disabilities* 24:330-342.

Englert, C.S., and T. Raphael. 1988. Constructing well-formed prose: Process, structure & metacognitive knowledge. *Exceptional Children* (April): 513-520.

Fawcett, S., and A. Sandbery. 1988. *Evergreen: A Guide to Writing.* Boston: Houghton Mifflin Company.

Frazier, D., and F.L. Paulson. 1992. How portfolios motivate reluctant writers. In *Performance Assessment*, ed. Ronald S. Brandt, 59-62. Alexandria: Association for Supervision and Curriculum Development.

Graham, S., C. Macarthur, S. Schwartz, and V. Page-Voth. 1992. Improving the compositions of students with learning disabilities using a strategy involving product and process goal setting. *Exceptional Children.* (February): 322-334.

Hanau, L. 1974. *The Study Game: How to Play and Win with Statement-PIE.* New York: Barnes and Noble.

Johnson, D., R. Johnson R., and E. Holubec. 1994. *Cooperative Learning in the Classroom.* Alexandria: The Association for Supervision and Curriculum Development.

Moran, M.R., J. Schumaker, J. and Vetter, A. 1981. Teaching a paragraph organization strategy to learning-disabled adolescents. Lawrence: University of Kansas.

Nichols, J. 1980. Using paragraph frames to help remedial high school students with written assignments. *Journal of Reading* 24 (3): 228-231.

Paulson, F.L., P.R. Paulson, and C.A. Meyer. 1992. What makes a portfolio a portfolio? In *Performance Assessment,* ed. Ronald S. Brandt, 51-54. Alexandria: Association for Supervision and Curriculum Development.

Rief, L. 1992. Finding the value in evaluation: Self-assessment in a middle school classroom. In *Performance Assessment.* Edited by Ronald S. Brandt, 45-48. Alexandria: Association for Supervision and Curriculum Development.

Scanlon, D., Duran, Reyes and Gillado. 1992. Interactive semantic mapping: An interactive approach to enhancing learning-disabled students' content area comprehension. *Learning Disabilities Research and Practice* 7 (3): 142-46.

Schumaker, J.B., S.M. Nolan, and D.D. Deshler. 1985. *The Error Monitoring Strategy.* Lawrence: University of Kansas Center for Research on Learning.

Stoddard, B. 1987. Teaching writing to learning-disabled students. *The Pointer.* 32 (1): 14-18.

Sullivan, K.E. 1980. *Paragraph Practice.* 4th ed. New York: MacMillan.

Vellecorsa, A., R. Ledford, and G. Parnell. 1991. Strategies for teaching composition skills to students with learning disabilities. *Teaching Exceptional Children*, 23 (2): 52-55.

Wallace, G., and D. Bott. 1989. Statement-PIE: A strategy to improve the paragraph writing skills of adolescents with learning disabilities. *Journal of Learning Disabilities* 22 (9): 541-553.

Wolf, D.P. 1992. Portfolio assessment: Sampling student work. *Performance Assessment,* ed. Ronald S. Brandt, 40-44. Alexandria: Association for Supervision and Curriculum Development.